Lots of love .
Baughan & Eileen .
Christmas 1992 .
X X .

The Country Child

AN ILLUSTRATED REMINISCENCE

This book contains many people's childhood memories, but they all occur in the same place. The world of childhood is timeless and common to us all. When we read Flora Thompson's well-documented historical account we feel not just interest but familiarity, we feel at home.

The reason for this becomes clear in Chapter Two: First Feelings where the writers recall the rare sensitivity with which we all first perceived our childhood world.

We felt, touched, tasted, smelled and saw things for the first time – uncompared. The vividness of these first perceptions draw us back, together, to impressions which, as 'archetypes, know no decay'.

Sudden penetrating childhood intuitions of exquisite beauty, or a fearful sense of dread, live on in minds which cannot help but return to them – in Chapter Three: The Spirit of Pan.

Then there are the simpler, Midsummer Joys of Chapter Four, which remind us why the sun always shone when we were young (though the games we once played, L P Hartley suggests, were not always what they seemed).

The Country Child is alive with ideas at the root of life. In the final chapter, we begin to see the power they exert as the child comes towards us once more in later life.

For the poet John Clare it is a fatal draw, but for others, like Henry Williamson and Beatrix Potter in their very different ways, it is their life's fulfilment.

'What heaven can be more real than to retain the spirit-world of childhood, tempered and balanced by knowledge and common sense, to fear no longer the terror that flieth by night, yet to feel truly . . .' *Beatrix Potter*

ACKNOWLEDGEMENTS

Typesetting, Reproduction and Printing
Typeset by Dorchester Typesetting Group Ltd, Dorset
Colour origination by Colour Trend, Singapore
Printed and bound in Great Britain by Richard Clay, Suffolk

Piers Dudgeon and Headline Book Publishing PLC would like
to thank all copyright holders for granting permission to print
and publish extracts from their works and photographs, in
which, in all cases, copyright is retained by them.

Text Acknowledgements
'Time and the Child' by Catherine Cookson, by kind
permission of Sheil Land Associates.
'Lark Rise to Candleford' by Flora Thompson (1945), by
kind permission of Oxford University Press.
'Cider with Rosie' by Laurie Lee, by kind permission of
Peters Fraser & Dunlop Group Ltd.
'A Boy in Kent' by C Henry Warren, originally published
by The Bodley Head Ltd, the Random Century Group.
'The Rabbit Skin Cap' by George Baldry, by kind
permission of Commander M E Cheyne.
'The Innocent Eye' by Herbert Read, by kind permission of
David Higham Associates Ltd.
'A Child Alone' and 'The Little Grey Men' by Denys
Watkins-Pitchford, by kind permission of David Higham
Associates Ltd.
'Autobiography' by Edwin Muir, by kind permission of
Chatto and Windus Ltd, the Random Century Group.
'A Cornish Childhood' by A L Rowse, by kind permission of
the author.
'The Country Child' by Alison Uttley, by kind permission of
Faber and Faber Ltd.
'Apostate' by Forrest Reid, by kind permission of John
Johnson (Author's Agent) Ltd.
'Surprised by Joy' by C S Lewis (1955), by kind permission
of HarperCollins Publishers.

'The House of Elrig' by Gavin Maxwell (© The Estate of
Gavin Maxwell Enterprises Ltd), by kind permission of
Gavin Maxwell Enterprises.
'The Autobiography of Arthur Ransome', edited by Rupert
Hart-Davis, by kind permission of the Random Century
Group Ltd.
'The Shrimp and the Anemone' by L P Hartley, by kind
permission of Miss Norah Hartley.
Works by Edmund Blunden, by kind permission of Peters
Fraser & Dunlop.
Works by Henry Williamson, by kind permission of A M
Heath & Co Limited.
Works by Beatrix Potter, by kind permission of Frederick
Warne Ltd, the Penguin Group.

Picture Acknowledgements
Peter Moyse; The Clays of Castle Top; Anthony Mott, the
Cornish Library; Jonathan Cape Ltd; Benedict Read; David
Higham Associates Ltd; Laurie Lee; The Victoria and
Albert Museum; Frederick Warne Ltd; Perth Museum &
Art Gallery; Cathie Beck, The Illustrated London News;
Nicola Oliver, The Tarka Project; Alexander Black, The
Wordsworth Museum; James and Gregory Stevens Cox,
Editors, The Thomas Hardy Yearbook, Guernsey; The
British Library; South American Pictures, Woodbridge,
Suffolk; Alison Fraser, The Orkney Library; Martin Collier,
The Norfolk Museums Service; Nuala la Vertue, The
Centre for Oxfordshire Studies, Oxfordshire County
Council Museum Services; The Mary Evans Picture
Library; The Institute of Agricultural History and Museum
of English Rural Life, University of Reading; The Hulton
Picture Company; Jim Lawson, The North of England
Open Air Museum, Beamish; Chris Volley, The Welholme
Galleries, Great Grimsby Borough Council; Ann Farr, The
Brotherton Collection, Leeds University Library; Dr Cane,
Bungay Museum; The Sutcliffe Gallery, Whitby; The Daily
Telegraph Magazine, Euan Macnaughton Associates.

The COUNTRY CHILD

Edited and with
original photography by
PIERS DUDGEON

HEADLINE

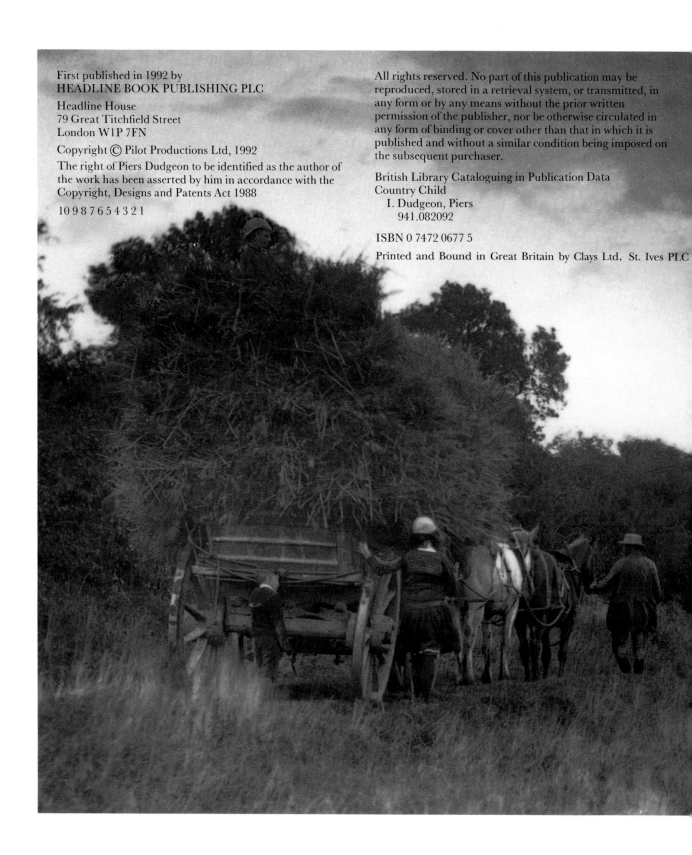

First published in 1992 by
HEADLINE BOOK PUBLISHING PLC

Headline House
79 Great Titchfield Street
London W1P 7FN

Copyright © Pilot Productions Ltd, 1992

The right of Piers Dudgeon to be identified as the author of
the work has been asserted by him in accordance with the
Copyright, Designs and Patents Act 1988

10 9 8 7 6 5 4 3 2 1

British Library Cataloguing in Publication Data
Country Child
    I. Dudgeon, Piers
        941.082092

ISBN 0 7472 0677 5

Printed and Bound in Great Britain by Clays Ltd, St. Ives PLC

CONTENTS

Millions who have read Catherine Cookson's memoir of her early years, 'Our Kate', will know that she grew up in difficult circumstances which later brought her to the brink of breakdown. Her success as a novelist may owe much to her successful resolution of this.

In 'Time and the Child', time is a circle, and the child she once was comes to meet her in later years. There is a sense of fulfilment imminent. It is what took many of the writers in this book back to the land of their childhood.

Catherine Cookson was born on June 20th, 1906, in sight of the gates of Tyne Dock which, in those days, was on the verge of the country. Up the hill from her grandfather's house were half a dozen big houses and above them a farm and a little country school and church.

TIME AND THE CHILD

When the race is almost run and the two ends of the circle are meeting you see the child coming towards you, and the knowledge of his magic is fresh before your eyes.
Catherine Cookson

I can smell my memories of childhood. The smell of real manure from a farmyard, as opposed to that from chemicals, recalls the scene of a farm outside Shields. I was on high ground. There were rocks and the sea to the left of me, and there away in the distance was a field of corn, red corn.

On closer investigation I found that the edge of the field was rimmed with fragile flowerheads, hundreds and hundreds of them. Kate, my mother, later told me they were called poppies. I thought the name didn't suit them somehow, they should have been called flamer; and there was no incongruity in the fact that this is what me granda called the people next door.

Perhaps it's old age creeping on or galloping on but I find my mind going back to these days to episodes in my childhood, more and more.

Here I am eighty-six and I know that inside I am still very much the child, the child that was Katie McMullen of East Jarrow, only the facade is the woman and it hasn't the power to control the child. Somehow I can't ignore the power of the child I once was and still am. I am still hurt as she was hurt. I still laugh as she laughed. I still have the secret insight that she had, the insight that recognised sorrow and loneliness in others, the insight – that was in me before I suckled milk, for, as our Kate said, if I in her womb had been aware of what she was suffering during those nine months that she carried me, then I should surely have been born mental.

Well, I must have been aware of her pain for I nearly went mental, didn't I?

I find that time is galloping away now; it isn't dawn before it's dusk. The hours leap into days and the days disappear into weeks, and I can't remember what I did in them. The pity of it is, my mind at this stage is clearer than at any period of my life, and I long for time, long time, the time of childhood, in which to expand and grow again.

You know, we are what our early environment makes us. I believe that is true. All through our life those early years colour our thinking. No matter how thick the veneer, heredity has a way of kicking itself through the skin. When the race is almost run and the two ends of the circle are meeting you see the child coming towards you, and you go back into his time more and more. You can recognise his thinking more so than when at twelve, thirteen or fourteen you left him behind. The knowledge of his magic is fresh before your eyes, for in his time of being there was no growing, there was no age. You knew people did what they called dying and although they were put into the earth they had gone into the sky; but you were here, there'd be new bread for tea, it was Saturday the morrow and there was no school. Sunday, you would have to go to Mass. On Monday. . . . When was Monday? There was no such thing as Monday, not on a Friday night. Monday wouldn't appear until late on Sunday night when you were dropping off to sleep. And Sunday was a long, long way off. It came after Saturday. But tonight was Friday and tomorow you would go to the penny matinee at The Crown. What greater joy could anyone ask for?

In that time I can smell baking day in the kitchen. I can see the kitchen as if it were set out before me. There's me sitting on the fender, Kate bustling all around me.

'Move your backside out of that,' she says.

I shuffle along the steel fender away from the black-leaded oven door, quickly past the fierce blazing fire built up in a slant you know to keep the heat against the oven, and when I reach the far end of the long fender I say, 'A . . . w!' for the steel is always cold between the end of me knickers and the top of me stockings.

I watch her lift the sneck of the oven door and pull out the oven shelf on which there are four loaf tins; she plonks the shelf onto the fender, dextrously upturns the loaf tins that are as black as the oven itself, gives three taps with her knuckles on the bottom of each tin, nods towards the oven as if acknowledging her debt to it, then looks at me and says, 'Have you got your yule-doo ready? Come on, look slippy if you want to put it in. I haven't got all day.'

I can see myself coming out of my dreaming, jumping to the table, picking up the much fingered piece of dough I've shaped into a man – perhaps this time he has currants for his eyes, mouth and nose, and a row for his coat, or perhaps this time funds were too low for currants and his face was featureless and his suit without buttons. I can see my laying him tenderly on the hot plate. I want to straighten him out, but Kate's voice will have none of it.

'Don't make a meal of it, not yet anyway. Out of me road!'

The oven door bangs on my yule-doo, Kate straightens her back, dusts the palms of her hands loudly against each other, blows a strand of hair from her sweating brow by thrusting out her lower jaw and puffing upwards, then she looks down on me and says gently, I can hear her saying it gently, 'Well, that's done, we'll have a sup tea, eh hinny?'

'Oh aye, Kate. Aye, yes.'

The smell of new bread slides me back into eternity, the eternity that was childhood; the eternity of pain and fear and that sick feeling in my chest caused by fear; the fear that me granda would make a big hole in his pay by dropping into the North-Eastern pub before coming home.

The fear that he might have had a very good week and so they'd all have a drop too much, and there'd be divils fagarties later on.

The fear there'd be no money on Monday for the rent; and I'd be kept off school to go to Bobs – Bobs was the pawnshop.

The fear that I'd have to miss Mass on Sunday 'cos me boots weren't decent.

The fear of facing the headmistress on the Monday and admit I hadn't been to Mass. Oh, that fear outdid the one of purgatory, hell and damnation.

But, as I said, there were moments of wonder when all these fears were forgotten in that everlasting time – by memories of flamers in a field, and the smell of new bread in that kitchen that served so many purposes, and the memory of which will stay with me till I die.

Chapter One: *Another Age*

**The past is a foreign country: they do things
differently there.**
L P Hartley

Flora Thompson

b. 1876

The hamlet stood on a gentle rise in the flat, wheat-growing north-east corner of Oxfordshire. We will call it Lark Rise because of the great number of skylarks which made the surrounding fields their springboard and nested on the bare earth between the rows of green corn.

All around, from every quarter, the stiff, clayey soil of the arable fields crept up; bare, brown and windswept for eight months out of the twelve. Spring brought a flush of green wheat and there were violets under the hedges and pussy-willows out beside the brook at the bottom of the 'Hundred Acres'; but only for a few weeks in later summer had the landscape real beauty. Then the ripened cornfields rippled up to the doorsteps of the cottages and the hamlet became an island in a sea of dark gold.

To a child it seemed that it must have always been so; but the ploughing and sowing and reaping were recent innovations.

Old men could remember when the Rise, covered with juniper bushes, stood in the midst of a furzy heath – common land, which had come under the plough after the passing of the Enclosure Acts.

Looking at the hamlet from a distance, one house would have been seen, a little apart, and turning its back on its neighbours, as though about to run away into the fields. It was a small grey stone cottage with a thatched roof, a green-painted door and a plum tree trained up the walls to the eaves. This was called the 'end house' and was the home of the stonemason and his family. At the beginning of the decade there were two children: Laura, aged three, and Edmund, a year and a half younger . . . After a break of five years, more babies had begun to arrive, and, by the end of the 'eighties, there were six children at the end house.

As they grew, the two elder children would ask questions of anybody and everybody willing or unwilling to answer them. Who planted the butter-cups? Why did God let the wheat get blighted? Who lived in this house before we did, and what were their children's names? What's the sea like? Is it bigger than Cottisloe Pond? Why can't we go to heaven in the donkey-cart? Is it farther than Banbury? And so on, taking their bearings in that small corner of the world they had somehow got into.

A cottage at Juniper Hill today, a survival from Flora Thompson's day, when none had more than two bedrooms and children of different sexes were segregated as to all the boys in one room and the girls in with their parents, where a screen or curtain was drawn as a partition.

The larks still rise over Juniper Hill, the place, near Oxford, where Laura's real-life persona, Flora Thompson, was born in 1876. It is an extraordinary experience walking out over the Rise soon after daybreak in May. The chattering and squealing of the skylarks is almost deafening as they play in the wind currents over the hamlet. It bestows immediate unshakeable credibility on Flora's three-part closely documented memoir, first published at a distance of some sixty years as 'Lark Rise', 'Over to Candleford', and 'Candleford Green'. The skylarks sing a song of continuity as well as change, as they once did for Flora, too:

All times are times of transition; but the eighteen eighties were so in a special sense, for the world was at the beginning of a new era, the era of machinery and scientific discovery.

Values and conditions of life were changing everywhere. Even to simple country people the change was apparent. The railways had brought distant parts of the country nearer; newspapers were coming into every home; machinery was superseding hand labour, even on the farms to some extent; food bought at shops, much of it from distant countries, was replacing the home-made and home-grown. Horizons were widening; a stranger from a village five miles away was no longer looked upon as 'a furriner'.

But side by side with these changes, the old country civilisation lingered. Traditions and customs which had lasted for centuries did not die out in a moment. State-educated children still played the old country rhyme games; women still went leazing . . . and men and boys still sang the old country

ballads and songs, as well as the latest music-hall successes.

'The old cocks don't like it when the young cocks begin to crow.' But, when the singing began they came into their own, for they represented the novel.

They usually had first innings with such songs of the day as had percolated so far. 'Over the Garden Wall', with its many parodies, 'Tommy, Make Room for Your Uncle', 'Two Lovely Black Eyes', and other 'comic' or 'sentimental' songs of the moment.

The men of middle age inclined more to long and usually mournful stories in verse, of thwarted lovers, children buried in snowdrifts, dead maidens, and motherless homes. Sometimes they would vary these with songs of a high moral tone, such as:

> Waste not, want not,
>   Some maxim I would teach;
> Let your watchword be never despair
> And practise what you preach.
>   Do not let your chances like the sunbeams pass you by,
> For you'll never miss the water till the well runs dry.

But this dolorous singing was not allowed to continue long. 'Now, then, all together, boys,' some one would shout, and the company would revert to old

'As they grew, the two elder children would ask questions of anybody and everybody willing or unwilling to answer them.'

'Words spoken and forgotten the next moment by the speaker were recorded in their memories, and the actions and reactions of others were impressed on their minds, until a clear, indelible impression of their little world remained with them for life.'

favourites. Of these, one was 'The Barleymow'.

> Oh, when we drink out of our noggins, my boys,
>   We'll drink to the barleymow.
> We'll drink to the barleymow, my boys,
>   We'll drink to the barleymow.
> So knock your pint on the settle's back;
>   Fill again, in again, Hannah Brown,
> We'll drink to the barleymow, my boys,
> We'll drink now the barley's mown.

So they went on, increasing the measure in each stanza from noggins to

half-pints, pints, quarters, gallons, barrels, hogsheads, brooks, ponds, rivers, seas, and oceans. That song could be made to last all evening . . .

There was a good deal of outdoor singing in those days. Workmen sang at their jobs; men with horses and carts sang on the road; the baker, the miller's man, and the fish-hawker sang as they went from door to door; even

The carter was at work an hour before the men appeared for work, getting the horses ready. 'With "Gee!" and "Wert up!" and "Who-a-a, now!" the teams would draw out . . . [and] with cracking of whips, clopping of

hooves and jingling of harness, the teams went tamping along the muddy byways . . . There were usually three or four ploughs to a field, each of them drawn by a team of three horses.'

the doctor and the parson on their rounds hummed a tune between their teeth. People were poorer and had not the comforts, amusements, or knowledge we have today; but they were happier. Which seems to suggest that happiness depends more upon state of mind – and body, perhaps – than upon circumstances and events.

'Shall we dance tonight or shall we have a game?'

How long the games had been played and how they originated no one knew, for they had been handed down for a time long before living memory and accepted by each generation as a natural part of its childhood.

One old favourite was 'Here Come Three Tinkers'. For this all but two of the players, a big girl and a little one, joined hands in a row, and the bigger girl out took up her stand about a dozen paces in front of the row with the smaller one lying on the turf behind her feigning sleep. Then three of the line of players detached themselves and, hand in hand, tripped forward, singing:

> Here come three tinkers, three by three,
> To court your daughter, fair ladye,
> Oh, can we have a lodging here, here, here?
> Oh, can we have a lodging here?

Upon which the fair lady (pronounced 'far-la-dee') admonished her sleeping daughter:

> Sleep, sleep, my daughter. Do not wake.
> Here come three tinkers you can't take.

Then, severely, to the tinkers:

> You cannot have a lodging here, here, here.
> You cannot have a lodging here.

And the tinkers returned to the line, and three others came forward, calling themselves tailors, soldiers, sailors, gardeners, bricklayers, or policemen, according to fancy, the rhymes being sung for each three, until it was time for the climax, and, putting fresh spirit into their tones, the conquering candidates came forward, singing:

> Here come three princes, three by three,
> To court your daughter fair ladye,
> Oh, can we have a lodging here, here, here?
> Oh, can we have a lodging here?

At the mere mention of the rank of princes the scene changed. The fair lady became all becks and nods and smiles, and, lifting up her supposedly sleeping daughter, sang:

> Oh, wake, my daughter, wake, wake, wake.
> Here come three princes you can take.

Occasionally, there'd be callers to the hamlet from far afield, their sudden appearance in striking contrast to the general lack of movement from one place to another usual in those days. In the summer a German band regularly showed up, stopping to play outside the inn, and one time, to their amazement, Laura and Edmund came face to face with a dancing bear.

'The man, apparently a foreigner, saw that the children were afraid to pass, and, to reassure them, set his bear dancing. With a long pole balanced across its front paws, it waltzed heavily to the tune hummed by its master, then shouldered the pole and did exercises at his word of command. The elders of the hamlet said the bear had appeared there at long intervals for many years; but that was its last appearance.'

And, turning to the princes:

> Oh, you can have a lodging here, here, here.
> Oh, you can have a lodging here.

Then, finally, leading forward and presenting her daughter, she said:

> Here is my daughter, safe and sound,
> And in her pocket five thousand pound,
> And on her finger a gay gold ring,
> And I'm sure she's fit to walk with a king.

In ten years' time the games would be neglected, and in twenty forgotten. But all through the 'eighties the games went on and seemed to the children themselves and to onlookers part of a life that always had been and always would be.

Very early in the morning, before daybreak for the greater part of the year, the hamlet men would throw on their clothes, breakfast on bread and lard, snatch the dinner baskets which had been packed for them overnight, and hurry off across fields and over stiles to the farm . . .

Harvest time was a natural holiday. 'A hemmed hard-worked 'n,' the men would have said; but they all enjoyed the stir and excitement of getting in the crops and their own importance as skilled and trusted workers, with extra beer at the farmer's expense and extra harvest money to follow.

The 'eighties brought a succession of hot summers and, day after day, as harvest time approached, the children at the end house would wake to the dewy, pearly pink of a fine summer dawn and the *swizzh, swizzh* of the early morning breeze rustling through the ripe corn beyond their doorstep.

Then, very early one morning, the men would come out of their houses, pulling on coats and lighting pipes as they hurried and calling to each other with skyward glances: 'Think weather's a-gooin' to hold?' For three weeks or more during the harvest the hamlet was astir before dawn and the homely odours of bacon frying, wood fires and tobacco smoke over-powered the pure, damp, earthy scent of the fields. It would be school holidays then and the children at the end house always wanted to get up hours before their time.

Awed, yet uplifted by the silence and clean-washed loveliness of the dawn, the children would pass along the narrow field paths with rustling wheat on

'We'll drink to the barleymow,' but not until after the harvest. At that time of year the favourite virtue was endurance: 'A man would say, "He says," says he, "that field o' oo-ats's got to come in afore night, for there's a rain a-comin. But we didn't flinch, not we! Got the last loo-ad under cover by midnight. A'moost too fagged-out to walk home, but we didn't flinch. We done it!"'

each side. Or Laura would make little dashes into the corn for poppies, or pull trails of the lesser bindweed with its pink-striped trumpets, like clean cotton frocks, to trim her hat and girdle her waist, while Edmund would stump on, red-faced with indignation at her carelessness in making trails in the standing corn.

In the fields where the harvest had begun all was bustle and activity. The scythe still did most of the work and they did not dream it would ever be superseded.

After the mowing and reaping and binding came the carrying, the busiest time of all. Every man and boy put his best foot forward then, for, when the corn was cut and dried it was imperative to get it stacked and thatched before the weather broke. All day and far into the twilight the yellow-and-blue painted farm wagons passed and repassed along the roads between the field and the stack-yard. Big cart-horses returning with an empty wagon were made to gallop like two-year-olds. Straws hung on the roadside hedges and many a gate-post was knocked down through hasty driving. In the fields men pitch-forked the sheaves to the one who was building the load on the

In those days, 'men were still mowing with scythes and a few women were still reaping with sickles.'

wagon, and the air resounded with *Hold tights*, and *Wert ups*, and *Who-o-oas*. The Hold tight! was no empty cry; sometimes, in the past, the man on top of the load had not held tight or not tight enough. There were tales of fathers and grandfathers whose necks or backs had been broken by a fall from a load, and of other fatal accidents afield, bad cuts from scythes, pitch-forks passing through feet, to be followed by lockjaw, and of sunstroke; but, happily, nothing of this kind happened on that particular farm in the 'eighties. At last, in the cool dusk of an August evening, the last load was brought in, with a nest of merry boys' faces among the sheaves on the top, and the men walking alongside with pitch-forks on shoulders. As they past along the roads they shouted:

> Harvest home! Harvest home!
> Merry, merry, merry harvest home!

and women came to their cottage gates and waved, and the few passers-by looked up and smiled their congratulations. The joy and pleasure of the labourers in their task well done was pathetic, considering their very small

'After the harvest had been carried from the fields, the women and children swarmed over the stubble picking up the ears of wheat the horse-rake had missed. Gleaning or "leazing", as it was called locally.' The corn would be thrashed out at home and ground into flour by the miller. In a good year, when leazing had been especially successful a family might keep the flour sack on show on a chair in the living-room – 'it was a common thing for a passer-by to be invited to "step inside an' see our little bit of leazings".'

share in the gain. But it was genuine enough; for they still loved the soil and rejoiced in their own work and skill in bringing forth the fruits of the soil, and harvest home put the crown on their year's work.

As they approached the farm-house their song changed to:

> Harvest home! Harvest home!
> Merry, merry, merry harvest home!
> Our bottles are empty, our barrels won't run,
> And we think it's a very dry harvest home.

and the farmer came out, followed by his daughters and maids with jugs and bottles and mugs, and drinks were handed round amidst general congratulations. Then the farmer invited the men to his harvest home dinner, to be held in a few days' time, and the adult workers dispersed to add up their harvest money and to rest their weary bones. The boys and youths, who could never have too much of a good thing, spent the rest of the evening circling the hamlet and shouting 'Merry, merry, merry harvest home!' until the stars came out and at last silence fell upon the fat rickyard and the stripped fields.

'The farmer came out, followed by his daughters and maids with jugs and bottles and mugs, and drinks were handed round amidst general congratulations.'

Laurie Lee

b. 1914

'Never to be forgotten, that first long secret drink of golden fire, juice of those valleys and of that time, wine of wild orchards, of russet summer, of plump red apples and Rosie's burning cheeks. Never to be forgotten, or ever tasted again.'

I was set down from the carrier's cart at the age of three; and there with a sense of bewilderment and terror my life in the village began.

The June grass, amongst which I stood, was taller than I was, and I wept. I had never been so close to grass before. It towered above me and all around me, each blade tattooed with tiger-skins of sunlight. It was knife-edged, dark and a wicked green, thick as a forest and alive with grasshoppers that chirped and chattered and leapt through the air like monkeys.

I was lost and didn't know where to move. A tropic heat oozed up from the ground, rank with sharp odours of roots and nettles. Snow-clouds of elder-blossom banked in the sky, showering upon me the fumes and flakes of their sweet and giddy suffocation. High overhead ran frenzied larks, screaming, as though the sky were tearing apart.

For the first time in my life I was out of the sight of humans. For the first time in my life I was alone in a world whose behaviour I could neither predict nor fathom: a world of birds that squealed, of plants that stank, of insects that sprang about without warning. I was lost and I did not expect to be found again. I put back my head and howled, and the sun hit me smartly on the face, like a bully. . .

'The June grass, amongst which I stood, was taller than I was, and I wept. I had never been so close to grass before.'

'The valley was narrow, steep and almost entirely cut off; it was also a funnel for winds, a channel for the floods, and a jungley, bird-crammed, insect-hopping sun-trap. . .'

The village to which our family had come was a scattering of some twenty to thirty houses down the south-east slope of a valley. The valley was narrow, steep and almost entirely cut off; it was also a funnel for winds, a channel for the floods, and a jungley, bird-crammed, insect-hopping sun-trap whenever there happened to be any sun. It was not high and open like the Windrush country, but had secret origins, having been gouged from the Escarpment by the melting ice-caps some time before we got there. The old flood-terraces still showed on the slopes, along which the cows walked sideways. Like an island, it was possessed of curious survivals – rare orchids and Roman snails; and there were chemical qualities in the limestone-springs which gave the women pre-Raphaelite goitres.

Nowhere is the secure cocoon of childhood better expressed than in Laurie Lee's remembrance of life in soft secluded Slad Valley during the second decade of the 20th Century.

It was a warm, sleepy, loving cocoon, which suited Laurie to a T, and Slad's sheltered valley community seemed lost to the changes of the world outside. 'Living down there,' he wrote, 'was like living in a bean-pod; one could see nothing but the bed one lay in.'

I was still young enough then to be sleeping with my mother, which to me seemed life's whole purpose. We slept together in the first-floor bedroom on a flock-filled mattress in a bed of brass rods and curtains. Alone, at that time, of all the family, I was her chosen dream companion, chosen from all for her extra love; my right, so it seemed to me.

So in the ample night and the thickness of her hair I consumed my fattened sleep, drowsed and nuzzling to her warmth of flesh, blessed by her bed and safety. From the width of the house and the separation of the day, we two then lay joined alone. That darkness to me was like the fruit of sloes, heavy and ripe to the touch. It was a darkness of bliss and simple langour, when all edges seemed rounded, apt and fitting . . .

My mother, freed from her noisy day, would sleep like a happy child, humped in her nightdress, breathing innocently, and making soft drinking sounds in the pillow. In her flights of dream she held me close, like a parachute to her back; or rolled and enclosed me with her great tired body so that I was snug as a mouse in a hayrick.

They were deep and jealous, those wordless nights, as we curled and muttered together, like a secret I held through the waking day which set me above all others . . .

The sharing of her bed at that three-year-old time I expected to last for ever. I had never known, or could not recall, any night spent away from her. But I was growing fast; I was no longer the baby; brother Tony lay in wait in his cot. When I heard the first whispers of moving me to the boys' room, I simply couldn't believe it. Surely my mother wouldn't agree? How could she face night without me? My sisters began by soothing and flattering; they said, 'You're a grown big man.' 'You'll be sleeping with Harold and Jack,'

The valley 'had secret origins, having been gouged from the Escarpment by the melting ice-caps some time before we got there. The old flood-terraces still showed on the slopes. . .'

'Living down there was like living in a bean-pod; one could see nothing but the bed one lay in.'

they said . . .

I was never recalled to my mother's bed again. It was my first betrayal, my first dose of ageing hardness, my first lesson in the gentle, merciless rejection of women.

I belonged to that generation which saw, by chance, the end of a thousand years' life. The change came late to our Cotswold valley, didn't really show itself till the late 1920s; I was twelve by then, but during that handful of years I witnessed the whole thing happen.

Myself, my family, my generation, were born in a world of silence; a world of hard work and necessary patience, of backs bent to the ground, hands massaging the crops, of waiting on weather and growth; of villages like ships in the empty landscapes and the long walking distances between them; of white narrow roads, rutted by hooves and cart-wheels, innocent of oil and petrol . . . the horse was king, and almost everything grew round him: fodder, smithies, stables, paddocks, distances and the rhythm of our days. His eight miles an hour was the limit of our movements, as it had been since the days of the Romans . . . This was what we were born to, and all we knew at first. Then, to the scream of the horse, the change began. The brass-lamped motor-car came coughing up the road, followed by the clamorous charabanc.

The first Choir Outing we ever had was a jaunt in a farm-wagon to Gloucester . . . Later, with the coming of the horse-brake and charabanc, the whole village took part as well.

The charabancs were high, with broad open seats and with folded tarpaulins at the rear, upon which, as choirboys, we were privileged to perch and to fall off and break our necks.

Slad wolf cubs. Laurie is standing second from left; village bully on the right.

In our file of five charabancs, a charioted army, we swept down the thundering hills. At the speed and height of our vehicles the whole valley took on new dimensions; woods rushed beneath us, and fields and flies were devoured in a gulp of air. We were windborne now by motion and pride, we cheered everything, beast and fowl, and taunted with heavy ironical shouts those unfortunates still working in the fields. . .

Mile after mile we went, under the racing sky, flying neckties and paper kites from the back, eyes screwed in the weeping wind. The elders, protected in front by the windscreen, chewed strips of bacon or slept. . .

The weather cleared as we drove into Weston-super-Mare, and we halted on the Promenade, 'The seaside,' they said: we gazed around us, but saw no sign of the sea. We saw a vast blue sky and an infinity of mud stretching away to the shadows of Wales. . . we boys just picked up and ran; we had a world of mud to deal with. . . Half the village now had hired themselves chairs and were bravely fighting the wind. Mrs Jones was complaining about Weston tea: 'It's made from drains, I reckon' . . . and the gravedigger (who appeared to have brought his spade) was out on the mud digging holes. Then the tide came in like a thick red sludge, and we all went on the pier.

One glided secretly to one's favourite machine, the hot coin burning one's hand, to command a murder, a drunk's delirium, a haunted grave or a Newgate hanging.

We spent more time on that turgid pier than anywhere else in Weston. Then the tide went out, and evening fell, and . . . we were all in our seats, the tarpaulin pulled over us, and with a blast of horns we left.

These appearances did not immediately alter our lives; the cars were freaks and rarely seen . . . we used the charabancs only once a year.

But the car-shying horses with their rolling eyes gave signs of the hysteria to come. Soon the village would break, dissolve and scatter, become no more than a place for pensioners. It had a few years left, the last of its thousand, and they passed almost without our knowing . . . Yet right to the end, like the false strength that precedes death, the old life seemed as lusty as ever.

The day Rosie Burdock decided to take me in hand was a motionless day of summer, creamy, hazy and amber-coloured, with the beech trees standing in heavy sunlight as though clogged with wild wet honey. It was the time of haymaking, so when we came out of school Jack and I went to the farm to help.

'The day Rosie Burdock decided to take me in hand was a motionless day of summer, creamy, hazy and amber-coloured. . . It was the time of haymaking.'

The whirr of the mower met us across the stubble, rabbits jumped like firecrackers about the fields, and the hay smelt crisp and sweet. The farmer's men were all hard at work, raking, turning and loading. Tall, whiskered fellows forked the grass, their chests like bramble patches. The air swung with their forks and the swathes took wing and rose like eagles to the tops of the waggons. The farmer gave us a short fork each and we both pitched in with the rest . . .

I stumbled upon Rosie behind a haycock, and she grinned up at me with the sly, glittering eyes of her mother. She wore her tartan frock and cheap brass necklace, and her bare legs were brown with hay-dust.

'Get out a there,' I said. 'Go on.'

Rosie had grown and was hefty now, and I was terrified of her. In her cat-like eyes and curling mouth I saw unnatural wisdoms more threatening than anything I could imagine. The last time we'd met I'd hit her with a cabbage stump. She bore me no grudge, just grinned.

'I got summat to show ya.'

'You push off,' I said.

I felt dry and ripping, icy hot. Her eyes glinted, and I stood rooted. Her face was wrapped in a pulsating haze and her body seemed to flicker with lightning.

'You thirsty?' she said.

'I ain't, so there.'

'You be,' she said. 'C'mon.'

So I stuck the fork into the ringing ground and followed her, like doom.

We went a long way, to the bottom of the field, where a wagon stood half-loaded. Festoons of untrimmed grass hung down like curtains all around it. We crawled underneath, between the wheels, into a herb-scented cave of darkness. Rosie scratched about, turned over a sack, and revealed a stone jar of cider.

'It's cider,' she said. 'You ain't to drink it though. Not much of it, any rate.'

Huge and squat, the jar lay on the grass like an unexploded bomb. We lifted it up, unscrewed the stopper, and smelt the whiff of fermented apples. I held the jar to my mouth and rolled my eyes sideways, like a beast at a waterhole. 'Go on,' said Rosie. I took a deep breath . . .

Never to be forgotten, that first long secret drink of golden fire, juice of those valleys and of that time, wine of wild orchards, of russet summer, of plump red apples and Rosie's burning cheeks. Never to be forgotten, or ever tasted again. . .

Rosie Burdock.

I put down the jar with a gulp and a gasp. Then I turned to look at Rosie. She was yellow and dusty with buttercups and seemed to be purring in the gloom; her hair was rich as a wild bee's nest and her eyes were full of stings. I did not know what to do about her, nor did I know what not to do. She looked smooth and precious, a thing of unplumbable mysteries, and perilous as quicksand.

'Rosie . . . ' I said, on my knees, and shaking.

She crawled with a rustle of grass towards me, quick and superbly assured. Her hand in mine was like a small wet flame which I could neither hold nor throw away. Then Rosie, with a remorseless, reedy strength, pulled me down from my tottering perch, pulled me down, down into her wide green smile and into the deep subaqueous grass.

Then I remember little, and that little, vaguely. Skin drums beat in my head. Rosie was close-up, salty, an invisible touch, too near to be seen or measured. And it seemed that the wagon under which we lay went floating away like a barge, out over the valley where we rocked unseen, swinging on motionless tides.

Then she took off her boots and stuffed them with flowers.

She did the same with mine. Her parched voice crackled like flames in my ears. More fires were started. I drank more cider. Rosie told me outrageous fantasies. She liked me, she said, better than Walt, or Ken, Boney Harris or even the curate. And I admitted to her, in a loud, rough voice, that she was even prettier than Betty Gleed. For a long time we sat with our mouths very close, breathing the same hot air. We kissed, once only, so dry and shy, it was like two leaves colliding in air.

C Henry Warren

b. 1880

'The invasion really had begun . . . I would hear them approaching along the woodland roads, scattering the quiet with their raucous voices.'

'The year revolved around the village, the festivals round the year, the Church round the festivals, the Squire round the Church, and the village round the Squire.' Laurie Lee writes of the old order of things. Slad village, when he was a boy, seemed to have its own momentum, unassailable by the outside world, though all the time it was spinning imperceptibly into the 20th Century. Paradoxically, Clarence Henry Warren's sense of the integrity of his village, Mereworth (pronounced, aptly, Merryworth) in Kent, was heightened by an annual invasion of it by aliens who turned the accepted order upside down.

The first of them came on foot, a dreary vanguard pushing perambulators heaped to twice their height with bulky bundles, a kettle and a saucepan clattering away somewhere underneath, and a tin bath piled on top.

Some came in wagons, singing. Perhaps I was playing somewhere in the lanes, between hedges bright with the changing maple. I would hear them approaching along the woodland roads, scattering the quiet with their raucous voices: and I do not know whether I was more filled with excitement at the novelty their arrival portended or with vague fear at the sudden intrusion of their loud ways . . .

Not many came in wagons: the majority, numbering several hundreds all told, came in trains that disgorged them at the next village, some two and a half miles away . . . in trains that boasted no cushions and obeyed no time-tables and spent the rest of the year patiently rotting in obscure sidings. When they had dragged their way up from the railway station, halting at every pub on the road, the invaders swarmed over Fladmere like ants, arrogant as conquerors, erasing the village's quiet and orderly habits clean out of existence, like a wet sponge over the neat handwriting of a child's slate. The new-comers tended to be irritable at first, wearied by a journey that had taken them the greater part of twenty-four hours and irked at finding themselves allotted insanitary huts with only straw to lie on and not even a fire to call their own. They would crowd into the shop, wanting bread, wanting oil, wanting groceries, and caustically impatient of delays. They would lean against Horace's barricade, tapping their coins on the counters and calling for immediate service. Horace was the odd-job man in the village. Warned of the invasion, he had arrived earlier at the shop 'with planks and poles and hammer and nails' and erected a high barricade around the counters.

The place rattled with his vigorous hammerings: the lamps shook and the dead wasps danced in the window. And when the barricade was ready, my father came along and hit it here and kicked it there to make sure it was strong enough to defend him and his assistants against the coming onslaught . . .

These, however, were only the last-minute preparations: less ostensibly, other parts of Fladmere had been getting ready for months. The village lay in the centre of the Kentish hop-growing district, and for nearly three-quarters of the year a large percentage of the land was bare save for a complicated system of poles and wires and string that netted the hop-gardens from hedge to hedge. No orchard trees were tended with half the care that Fladmere devoted to its hop-bines. As soon as they appeared out of the ground, the tender shoots were nursed and pinched and thinned. Men on long stilts picked their way down the narrow alleys between the poles, tightening the cross-pieces of wire and threading the miles of manila string that was needed to carry each slender bine from earth to sky.

Of all these complicated preparations the invaders themselves neither knew nor cared. Mostly they came from the East End of London, and Fladmere meant little more to them than an outlandish place somewhere in the country, where the inhabitants were terribly slow, where bulls might be met with unexpectedly in the fields, and where in September you could earn good money picking hops . . . For four or five weeks they would work by day in the hop-gardens and sleep by night in the huts and tents provided for them by the farmers. In between times there would be a great deal of noisy fun.

. . . The old-timers took everything as it came. After ten or even twenty Septembers, they had learned to suffer Fladmere's country ways with an easy tolerance, even glad to find it unchanging . . . [and] they would banter with my father, very conscious of the superiority of cockney over country wit.

There was, for instance, Mrs Grunter – Eliza, as everybody called her. She would roll into the shop like a gargantuan sack, tied not too securely round the middle. She oozed laughter. She had little black eyes that shone out of the deep folds of her face, always brimming over with tears. On the day of her arrival she wore a black satin coat that came down to her heels, and her hair, screwed into a tight 'bun' at the back, was surmounted uneasily by a bonnet that waved a purple osprey plume as she laughed. But from that day onwards, she discarded bonnet and coat, and appeared in an old shawl, one corner of which was always trailing along the ground, while her 'bun' perpetually escaped in an untidy tangle of tails down her back. Like the rest of the invaders, Eliza looked upon the country as a place to unbutton and relax in.

''Ere we are agen, ol' dear!' she would say. 'An' ain't you sorry to see us: not 'alf you ain't! Rattlin' in the profits faster than we can rattle 'ops off the bine. Oh, don't tell me! Now, 'ow much is that bit of fat bacon over there? Gawd! You don't 'alf shove the prices up when you see me comin' – AND you don't need a telescope, neither.' Turning to her companion, a newcomer, she continued: 'Still, 'e ain't a bad ol' dear, take 'im all round – *all* round, I said!'

Or there was Long Tom, who stood six feet four in his almost soleless

'The hop-harvest is a godsend to East-End Londoners, and this season they will be glad enough to get out of the pale of the water-famine.' So wrote a reporter for The Sketch *in 1898. A year earlier, the sheer number of children in the hop-gardens was noted. While one boy, aged nine, had picked two bushels by 11 am, and 'will probably manage five before the day is out, which, this years, brings him one shilling,' others happily snoozed the day away, apparently soothed by the hop vapour (hop pillows were then widely used for insomniacs).*

boots and was as thin as a hop-pole. Rags fluttered from him as from a scarecrow. He stuttered painfully and wrung his hands all the while. With every word he would roll his tongue round his lips, whistle, and seem to be trying to tie his jaw into knots. Fortunately, he spoke very little, but would reach a lean, dirty hand over the heads of the other customers and give in his order on a slip of paper. The writing was almost indecipherable. 'What! Another billy-do?' some wit would call out, as my father held the crumpled scrap up to the light. 'Come on, mister! Don't keep us 'ere all night: there's duck an' green peas waitin' for us back at the 'uts!' But my father persevered, and at last Long Tom was served and allowed to thin away through the crowd like a ghost . . . Only twice throughout the season did I hear him speak at any length: on the day of his arrival and on the day of his departure. On this last occasion he would slide up to the counter, seize my father's hand, and begin most laboriously to tell his pleasure at having seen us all again . . . not until the last painful word was spoken did he loosen his clammy grip. Even my father's ingenious good humour was often hard put to find the suitable reply; but I could detect a catch in his voice afterwards, when he said: 'I wonder what hole he'll hide in till hopping comes round again?' Long Tom haunted my dreams many a night after hop-picking was finished and done with.

Once the strangers (as we called them, to differentiate them from the home pickers) had settled themselves in their huts and tents, they took complete possession of Fladmere. They were respecters neither of persons nor things . . . they roamed about at will, breaking branches off trees, soiling everywhere, and scattering their refuse over the countryside. The local

'Their homes are sometimes low-roofed white cottages, sometimes wooden huts, and sometimes the old military tents of the hoppers' camp. In these last they are soon sound asleep on beds of straw. . .'

In fact there was little that was quaint about the purpose-built huts in the hoppers' camps. The crumbling ruins of some may still be seen today in a neighbouring village to Mereworth. Rows of brick walled, corrugated iron roofed, 10-foot square, windowless, numbered rooms were available, one per family, as shelter for the straw beds. Yet some villages today still receive holiday-makers doing pilgrimage in honour of the countless earlier generations of their families that came, annually, to stay in them.

When first published, in 1898, this picture was captioned, The Sunday Dinner. *That year it was estimated that 50,000 hoppers invaded Kent. 'Most of the harvesters go down into Kent by train. But others are so poor that they must needs tramp it by foot,' read the accompanying article.*

policeman was quite unable to do anything about it . . . But when it came to stripping bines there were few home pickers who could beat them. With the cumbersome bines thrown across their knees, they sat tearing off the flaky hops in handfuls, letting them fall in a green cascade until the bin was packed to the brim and would hold no more . . . Presently a voice would shout down the leafy alleys: 'Get your hops ready!' . . . And when at last the cleaning was finished, there was nothing to do but to sit around and sing. This way I learned all the popular songs of the day, from 'Down at the ol' Bull an' Bush' to ''Twas only a Bewtiful Picture in a Bewtiful Golden Frame.' Timidly the home pickers would join in the singing round the bins, their more genteel efforts drowned beneath the surge and swell of lusty cockney voices . . .

The measurer appeared and a hush fell on the pickers. We who lived in Fladmere knew him best as Dickie, the sexton and gravedigger; and I for one never ceased to be astonished at the change that had come over him . . . He cursed the strangers up hill and down dale, calling them 'lousy Londoners', 'b----y foreigners', and far worse, as though he hated them and revelled in his brief power over them . . .

Then there was the 'Bookie' who, in ordinary life, was the village schoolmaster. But whereas the sexton gained in authority at this season, the schoolmaster lost: as 'Bookie' he was not only Dickie's inferior but had to suffer the further indignity (under the eyes of his pupils, too) of acting as butt for those caustic sallies which the pickers were afraid to hurl at their real enemy. His black moustache was spiked and twirled as imposingly as ever. His clothes were of a cut and cloth far above anybody else's. And he totted up the bushels in his book with a dash that proclaimed at once the superiority of his profession. But none of these things could restore to him that awful dignity which was his throughout the year. He was even further

Tallying up at the end of the day. Young Henry was 'too much of a spectator' for his own liking – his parents forbad him to run loose in the hop-gardens. But when sufficient hops had been picked for the day, and a voice shouted down the lines, 'Get your hops ready!' it was a signal to find his way in and sit round with the hoppers and listen to them sing.

Then the measurer appeared, and a mighty hush fell.

demeaned in our eyes because he wore a schoolboy's canvas satchel slung across his back, for the easier carrying of his books.

Seeing the men and women of Mereworth through the eyes of the invaders might have made Henry question the order of things in his little world. But as soon as they left, everything and everyone resumed their safe and normal positions, and the natural rhythm of day-to-day life, set off in the fragile time around dawn by George, the baker, whistling to himself as he thumped the dough in the bakery beneath Henry's bedroom window, settled back into its customary swing.

George Baldry

b. 1864

'Many a genius must have come into the world his father following at the plough's tail and followed in his footsteps, on the same farm.'

Flora Thompson found her way up and out of Juniper Hill. Idyllic as her life may sound, it suited the child but not the adult. For many, however, born in the country of working stock in the last third of the 19th Century, there was no such movement, as George Baldry recalls in his memoir, 'The Rabbit Skin Cap'.

Reading Flora Thompson's 'harvest home' makes you wonder why she or George or any of these country children would want to escape.

The truth is, life was hard; money was scarce, and for some, an education was seen as inappropriate.

As a boy, George had only one pair of trousers and those were ragged and patched. His diet was meagre, breakfast was 'skim milk and a piece of bread', or salt soap – 'a few pieces of bread crumbled into a basin with small pieces of butter, lard, or dripping with hot water poured over, the water dipped up out of the river, making our sop like good broth with bubbles of fat floating on top. A few bits of weed and an insect or two didn't matter to us . . . My brother got fat on it but I was that poor and skinny I was nicknamed 'Bones'. If my parents could have fed us better they would have done, but we had to live on whatever we could get.'

Nor was George lucky in school.

I was born in the Loke, six-fifty-seven on a Saturday evening so I've heard my parents say, coming into the world the time the bells of St Mary's Church, Bungay, were tolling in for service. I've lived within sound of them bells all my days, for all that I live in Ditchingham in the county of Norfolk, and Bungay is over the border in Suffolk, this village being half in one and half in t'other as one might say, the river Waveney running between.

Grandfather was born in 1800 and went to work as a boy of eight year old on a farm. What with short vittals and hard work he grew that shambly the men called him 'Hoggity-hoy he's not a man nor yet a boy!' but he never took no notice and was soon as big as any on 'em.

Being allus in the open he never had a day's illness in his life. He walked two miles to his work every day and had a family of eight children to keep, of which my mother was one. To help bring in a living he had a couple of cows and a few pigs and fowls, and my grandmother looked to them and made sheepskin gloves and buskins [gaiters] by candlelight at night.

She used to have to walk twelve miles to get the supply of leather and

The Mill House. 'My father took over as tenant going in Michaelmas, 1869 . . . It felt strange to see so many trees and a big river running just a'low my bedroom winder.'

trudge home with it herself. That way they managed well enough till the family was growed up and out in the world. One autumn afternoon when she was gettin' on in years she picks up the 'slings' or bucket yoke and away to milk the cows out grazin' on the Common. The bounders had strayed – she was a long time a'gettin' them up, and by the time they was milked it was day-end, and a fog with it thick as a feather bed. She missed her way among the dykes and wandered all night, not knowing which way to turn, still a-carrying the milk pails, and when dawn come found herself right over by Bungay. She got home six o'clock time, exhausted – and died two hours after.

Through her loss my grandfather lost heart – couldn't abide the place no longer, sold the cows and pigs and went to live with an old friend of his. My father took over his place as tenant going in Michaelmas, 1869, and that's how we came to the Mill House.

I was then nearly four years of age and can picture it now in my mind, going for the first time down the long drive holding my mother's hand, and saying, 'Where do we go?' not knowing then that there was a turn that led across the medder to the house, and could not make it out, nor where I was being led to. Had not been there long a'fore I begin to pipe my eye and cry out wanting to be back agin to my old home, little knowing it was going to be my home for life.

It felt strange to see so many trees and a big river running just a'low my bedroom winder. I went to bed and the wind was blowing hard, making the trees moan and rattle and scaring me so that I blared for my Mother and she soon told me what the racket was and tuck me up close, and I laid as quiet as a mouse till morning.

After a bit of breakfast Mother turned me out with my sister and brother to play on the medder, saying 'Don't you go near that river – du you du I'll thrash you.' We did not, never having seen one before, the look was enough, but when we got used to the place playing round the river become a wonder

'Many a genius must have come into the world his father following at the plough's tail and followed in his footsteps, on the same farm . . . only known to have lived by his family.'

to us, and the ducks and the water hens made us long to get on it ourselves, but this wasn't to Mother's liking. She told us to keep playing on the medder but somehow the pull of the water drew us back to it again.

In most country places the working men and women stayed in the village they were born in, and was reared according to the family tradition. Many a genius must have come into the world his father following at the plough's tail and followed in his footsteps, on the same farm. Seeing the sun casting its shadow as it rose in the East going to work, toiling on till it set in the West. Growing from boyhood, blooming into manhood with his breast full of that spirit and creative instinct with which nature endowed him, but no learning and no chance to go out into the world to better hisself, rooted deep down in the soil, till at last he go feet first the way of all men, only known to have lived by his family and the farmer he worked for.

There's a rhyme used to be on a stone that lay in the churchyard which the old folk said had been took out of the Church when the heating were put in which I always thought spoke the truth about most of us – ran this way.

> Without a name forever senseless, dumb
> Dust only now contains this silent tomb,
> Where 'twas I lived or died it matter not.
> To whom related, or by whom begot.
> I was but am not, ask no more of me,
> T'is all I am, and all that you must be.

June 4th, 1871, we sets out to school for the first time, I being six years and seven months old, my sister eighteen months older than me and my brother Billy fifteen months younger.

Mother tells us to be careful crossing the road, but 'twasn't likely we'd meet more than a horse and cart and a wheelbarrow, so we gits there safe and sound and were put on a form in the infants' room. While prayers were said we were gaping at all the boys and girls and feeling very shy.

The Teacher give us each a slate and pencil and tells us to look at the blackboard and the letters she was a-chalking and copy 'em on our slates. We does the best we could, but Teacher with an eye like a hawk soon sees I'm using my left hand, and I get a rap on the knuckles for doing it. We goes out to play and I gits pushed over and starts howling till she comes over and picks me up, and back we goes and does some more scribbling.

We goes home for dinner and Mother says she misses us cruel, couldn't ha' believed she would, and my sister tells how that boy George would keep using his left – and Teacher hit him – and if that wasn't silly enough he must git pushed and fall down rushing about at play-time. Then Father says: 'That'll du, I don't want to hear no more,' and when Father spoke out we knew what that meant and shoves down our dinners and off back to school.

I soon tumbles to it and gets on all right and could write the alphabet from the blackboard and was put on the top seat of the gallery with the best scholars in the infant room.

It was easy there to see if I used my left hand, but one day when I thought she weren't looking I changed the pencil over and soon had my copy done. Teacher sees and calls out: 'Put that pencil in your right hand, young Baldry, if I catch you using your left hand again I'll give you the cane.' And I says: 'My mother uses her left hand, why shan't I?'

I didn't make much progress using my right hand and my copy was allus being crossed off, so whenever I see a chance I'd slip the pencil into my left hand, keeping one eye on the Teacher, and soon she twigged me. She called out for me to come down from the gallery as she had something to show me, so of course I was down in a crack, and only when she pulled out the cane

'June 4th, 1871, we sets out to school for the first time. Mother tells us to be careful crossing the road, but wasn't likely we'd meet more than a horse and cart and a wheelbarrow.'

did I see what it was I was to see. Twisting up her lip she told me to hold out my hand and down it come but I was quicker and the cane come down on her knee. Then she got the wind up – called one of the assistants to hold me – and she caught my wrist and let me have it – one – two – three – four , and some extra to make up for the one she missed. Then there was a storm of tears and blubbering – the rest of the Class sat as quiet as mice – and the Teacher took no more notice, feeling sure I wouldn't use my left hand again. Nor did I, for it was so sore and tingling for days after it cured me for life of writing with it, though there's many a job to this day I'd sooner use my left hand for.

One night Father asks how I be a-getting on at school, and what they have learnt me, and can I count this way?

A ha-penny wet and a ha-penny dry
Fourpence ha-penny and a ha-penny by
A ha-penny behind and a ha-penny before
Fourpence ha-penny and a ha-penny more.

'There yew are, boy – count that up then I shall know is you be a-larnin' ought at school.'

I went outside, as I knew where some gravel lay, picked up two small stones, called 'em four farthings, then four big 'uns – called 'em one penny each, that made five pennies, four more small ones that made one penny, counted 'em up they made six altogether. Though if there be six in one half the other must be the same, twice six is twelve, that's a bob. In I go pleased as punch and Father asks if I had a-counted 'em yet.

'Yes, that I have,' says I.

'Lay yer a penny yew h'aint.'

'I know I hev – that's a bob, that is – give me yer penny.'

'No! No! Boy, you niver laid yer penny down.'

'I won, Father, you knows I have – give us it.'

'I'll be blowed, boy, yew've cost me pennies enough and I can see yew ha' been to school long enough for the likes of us. I'll find yew a job afore yew git too much learnin' and start a-runnin' round yer betters all ways, shan't know what to du with yer. I'll have yer at work come spring time else my name's not Happy Jack.'

It was then November and not for me to choose.

In the end, like many other children of farm labourers, George Baldry's education was, by default, effectively undertaken in the fields. When first he arrived at the Mill House he knew nothing of nature at all, but soon left and right hand are successfully engaged in activities to which the world had dictated he was born. And that river – it, too, had lessons in store for the growing boy:

Harvest time was near and we was looking forward to running rabbits in the big field. I thought if I could git a piece or two of Father's herring netting

George Baldry and his wife.

and put over some of the holes along the fence, the rabbits'd draw away there as the field would cut.

Away come ten harvesters with their scythes on their shoulders – no reaping machines then – and start mowing by the field gate. I slips round to the other end with my netting ready hid up and puts it over the most likely holes I thought they would bolt into, laying it loose over a stick to keep it from being pulled inside. Then I hides in the fence well under cover, armed with a short stick.

The cutters come along up the top end of the field and started a-shouting, 'Lo-lo-lo' – and bounce come a fat rabbit into my net. Had it in a moment and taps him sharp behind the ears with the side of my palm which soon finished him, that being the only right way to kill a rabbit – done in a second. Wasn't long afore another slips out of the standing corn and into one of my holes and I soon had him. Then I hid 'em both up in different places, as I heard my mother say, 'He who hides can find.'

The reapers begun to work round by my end of the field then, so I had to be careful. If they'd caught me it would have been goodbye – a clout on the ear and the toe of the shoemaker's boot for me. Soon there was a only a long strip standing and the rabbits started running hard out of the last bit o' corn. I gits six afore I finished and then thinks the reapers being so close this is the one the cobbler threw at his wife [the last] and packs up and off home with a rabbit stuffed into the front of my trousers.

So I went bakkard and forrard fetched the lot and stowed 'em in an old rabbit locker at home . . .

Father bring me a doe that night – a tame 'un – and was fair surprised to find the locker full o' rabbits. When I tells him what I done he laughs and says I was darn lucky and did I bring the netting home and not get found out? When he finds that's all right, he says how did I get 'em home? and I says: 'In the tops of my trousers,' – plenty of room – as they's made out of hissen.

He laughs some more, and so do Mother, and she give him a look and say, 'It's sartin shure he ought to be able to catch a rabbit now he's got father's trousers on.'

We had a good blow out from them rabbits which fill up Father's old trousers so tight there wasn't no more room to put a rabbit down the front.

'It won't be long afore I'll git one if they're good to eat.'

> I might advert
> To numerous accidents in flood or field,
>   . . . tragic facts
> Of rural history that impressed my mind
> With images, to which in following years
> Far other feelings were attached, with forms
> That yet exist with independent life
> And, like their archetypes, know no decay.
> *from 'The Prelude' by William Wordsworth*

Father said, 'Cock Robin was crying the Sweep's Old Woman.' (He being the Town Crier of Bungay, as well as a Rag Merchant.) So I scuttles off to listen and sure enough there he was making the winders shake with his bellowing – 'Early this morning while our worthy town sweep was on duty up a flue his old girl Susan wearing a crinoline, black stockings and poke bonnet become lost, stolen or strayed. She wake up and see her husband lying black with soot by her side and her reason being gone astray did think he was the devil himself sleeping beside her. When he returned home his wife had runned away. All who bring news of her dead or alive will be rewarded.'

I remember standing there and listening to the women round wagging their heads and saying, 'Poor dear, poor thing, if they finds her she'll be took away for sure. It's in the river she is, I'll be bound.'

Coming home across the bridge what should I see but two men in a boat a'pulling at something in the water with boat-hooks – something that rolled over when they touched it and a bit of black skirt which was blowing out with the air under it. I didn't see no face nor nothing, but I takes to me heels and runs home as fast as I could lay feet on the ground with a cold feeling in the pit of my stomach. I said nothing to nobody, but all my days I have remembered that bit of black skirt blowing out of the muddy water, for child as I was, it was then I begun to realise what us poor humans can be druv to, when things go amiss.

Chapter Two: *First Feelings*

**The mind of man is fashioned and built up
Even as a strain of music.**
William Wordsworth

Herbert Read

b. 1893

'The only real experiences in life [are] those lived with a virgin sensibility.'

The wild North Yorkshire moors, and 'narrow wooded dales which strike like green rays into the purple darkness' – the northern shore of a primaeval lake which, when the waters had drained away, became the flat-bottomed Vale where the Reads' isolated farmhouse lay.

Sir Herbert Read was a cultured man, a poet published by the time he was twenty-two, Professor of Fine Art at Edinburgh in his thirties, a critic, novelist, and a personal prose writer of supreme refinement, yet he was born with no greater expectations than George Baldry, on a modest isolated farm called Muscoates Grange in a flat wide-bottomed vale beneath the wild North Yorkshire moors.

The farmhouse: 'a square stone box with a roof of vivid red tiles', to its left the outhouses containing saddle-room, shed and blacksmith's shop.

Struck by the anachronism, the novelist and critic Graham Greene wrote, 'A whole world of the imagination seems to separate the rather dry sophisticated critic from the vale, the orchard, the foldgart, the mill and the stackyard – the fine simple stony architecture of his childhood.'

Read's autobiography to ten years of age, 'The Innocent Eye', Greene called 'one of the finest evocations of childhood in our language'. It is about to be re-published, an event long overdue. Read's purpose in writing it seems to have been to open the shutters of memory and rediscover 'those images of truth' which lie at the heart of creative imagination.

If only I can recover the sense and uncertainty of those innocent years, years in which we seemed not so much to live as to be lived by forces outside us, by the wind, the trees, the moving clouds and all the mobile engines of our expanding world – then I am convinced I shall possess a key to much that has happened to me in this other world of conscious living. The echoes of my life which I find in my early childhood are too many to be dismissed as vain coincidences; but it is perhaps my conscious life which is the echo, the only real experiences in life being those lived with a virgin sensibility – so that we only hear a tone once, only see a colour once, see, hear, touch, taste and smell everything but once, the first time. All life is an echo of our first sensations, and we build up our consciousness, our whole mental life, by variations and combinations of these elementary sensations.

The vale where the Reads lived, contained, millennia ago, a fresh water lake released by the action of the sea eroding the hills to the east, hence its flatness today – as flat as once had been the surface of the lake. The farmhouse is described in 'The Innocent Eye' as 'a square stone box with a roof of vivid red tiles', set towards the western end of the valley, six miles from Helmsley, the nearest town. In front of the kitchen door lay an acre of green. Facing the house, to its left, outhouses contained saddle-room, shed and blacksmith's shop; to its right a long range of sheds followed the path to the kitchen door; and so on.

I had a clear idea of each province of the house and land before I arrived and wasn't disappointed. Asking the way I was warned that I'd never be able to understand the dialect of the people living there now – a farm worker and his wife, 'plain people'. I was undeterred, suspecting that, however 'plain' they may appear to locals, Read's successors at Muscoate Grange probably read Virgil in their spare time.

I had a fine reception. The farm wife who answered the door found me checking that everything, bar the pump and the elms by the pond, were indeed still in place, and allowed me into the kitchen. The fireplace I knew to have been on the right as one

The 'velvet stillness' of the flat fields stretching away from the farm.

enters, and so it is, as are so many of the dimensions accurately recalled by Read at a distance of more than thirty-five years.

Maybe it was because he had travelled so far that the architecture of this, his distant starting place, remained strangely coherent in his mind's eye. This was the room, with its long deal table, its old oak dresser on the left as you enter, its stone-flagged floor, its beamed ceiling groaning with bacons and hams, that was the daily scene of 'intense bustle':

The kitchenmaid was down by five o'clock to light the fire; the labourers crept down in stockinged feet and drew on their heavy boots; they lit candles in their horn lanthorns and went out to the cattle. Breakfast was at seven, dinner at twelve, tea at five. Each morning of the week had its appropriate activity: Monday was washing day, Tuesday ironing, Wednesday and Saturday baking, Thursday 'turning out' upstairs and churning, Friday 'turning out' downstairs. Every day there was the milk to skim in the dairy . . .

At dinner, according to the time of the year, there would be from five to seven farm labourers, the two servant girls, and the family, with whom, for most of the time, there was a governess – a total of from ten to fifteen mouths to feed every day. The bustle reached its height about midday; the men would come in and sit on the dresser, swinging their legs impatiently; when the food was served they sprang to the benches and ate in solid gusto, like animals. They disappeared as soon as the pudding had been served, some to smoke a pipe in the saddle room, others to do work that could not wait. Then all the clatter of washing up rose and subsided. More peaceful occupations filled the afternoon. The crickets began to sing in the hearth. The kettle boiled for tea. At nightfall a candle was lit, the foreman or the shepherd sat smoking in the armchair at the fireside end of the table. The latch clicked as the others came in one by one and went early to bed.

As I emerged from the farmhouse, I looked beyond the Foldgarth to the Stackyard where the great festival was threshing time:

Late one afternoon we would hear the chuff and rattle of the engine and threshing machine far away on the high-road, and away we would race to meet it. The owner of the engine, Jabez by name, was a great hero in the eyes of children . . . We would run across the Green and find round the corner the most exciting scene of the year. The engine stood before us, merry with smoke and steam; the big fly-wheel winked in the sunlight; the bright balls of the revolving 'governor' (Jabez had taught me the technical names) twinkled in a minor radiance. Jabez was in the cabin stoking the glowing furnace. The big leather belt swung rhythmically between the fly-wheel and the threshing-machine. Two men on the top of a stack threw down the sheaves; two others cut them open and guided then into the monster's belly; the monster groaned and gobbled, and out of its yammering mouth came the distracted straw; elsewhere emerged the prickly chaff and below, into sacks that reached the ground, trickled the precious corn. A cloud of dust and

'Late one afternoon we would hear the chuff and rattle of the engine and the threshing machine . . . and away we would race to meet it.'

'By the bridge was a pool with a projecting pier; this was the sheep-dip, where annually the sheep were given some kind of antiseptic bath.'

chaff swirled round everything. As the stack disappeared, and approached ground-level, we were armed with sticks and the dogs became attentive and expectant. The last layer of sheaves was reached; out raced the rats which had made a home in the bedding of thorn on which the stack rested, and then for a few minutes the Stackyard was an abode of demons: dogs barked, men and children shouted in a lust of killing, and the unfortunate rats squealed in panic and death agonies. Sometimes we found a nest of newly-born rats, and then we were suddenly sad.

In reality, the day I was there, the farmyard and huge open valley space was as quiet as Read described it when work ceased and the day drew to a close one hundred years ago. I could imagine how surely, amidst the 'velvet stillness' of these fields, a boy's ear would be attuned at the dead of night to the subtlest sounds. A cow lowing in the field, the clatter of horses' hooves on the nearby road.

But one thing confused me – the site of the copper-house where the clothes were boiled on a Monday. Read described it as being behind the pump, handy to the water, but there was no longer a pump and my guide was no help. The copper-house stuck in my mind because what happened outside it, and annually on every farm, was recalled with horror by more than one country child grown old. For Flora Thompson it was a scene 'with its mud and blood, flaring lights and dark shadows . . . as savage as anything to be seen in an African jungle.' Alison Uttley would retire 'to the top of the house where she lay with her fingers in her ears, weeping and sick with misery' rather than attend its unwelcome occurrence. For Edwin Muir in the wilds of the Orkneys, it was yet one more scene in the 'carnival of life and death' that characterises farm-life. Herbert Read's own passive reaction to it, however, was to convince him that childhood innocence was characterised by a marked lack of sentiment.

Alison Uttley recalled being sad even when she went to the circus as a young child – the elephants 'were like Samson in the hands of the Philistines, poor giants captive, waiting for God to tell them to pull down the tent poles and bury the crowd in its fold.'

The divergence in reaction to farmyard horror was one of the themes batting around my head at the time. Is it simply that girls are more squeamish than boys? Does it raise the whole question of how much of how we feel as very young children is truly replicated in adult memory, and how much recalled through a veil of civilising influences? Or, does it, as Read suspects, tell us something fundamental about our 'virgin sensibilities'.

Outside the copper-house the pigs were killed, to be near the cauldron of boiling water with which they were scalded. The animal was drawn from its sty by a rope through the ring in its nose: its squealing filled the whole farm till it reached the copper-house, and there by the side of a trestle its throat was cut with a sharp knife and the hot blood gushed on to the ground. The carcass was then stretched on the trestle, and the whole household joined in the work of scraping the scalded hide: it was done with metal candlesticks,

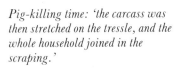

Pig-killing time: 'the carcass was then stretched on the tressle, and the whole household joined in the scraping.'

the hollow foot making a sharp and effective instrument for removing the bristles and outer skin. The carcass was then disembowelled and dismembered. The copper was once more requisitioned to render down the surplus fat, which was first cut into dice. The remnants of this process, crisp shreds known as scraps, formed our favourite food for days afterwards. In fact, pig-killing was followed by a whole orgy of good things to eat – pork-pies, sausages and pigs'-feet filling the bill for a season. But the scenes I have described, and many others of the same nature, such as the searing of horses' tails, the killing of poultry, the birth of cattle, even the lewdness of a half-witted labourer, were witnessed by us children with complete passivity – just as I have seen some children of the same age watching a bull-fight in Spain quite unmoved by its horrors. Pity, and even terror, are emotions which develop when we are no longer innocent, and the sentimental adult who induces such emotions in the child is probably breaking through defences which nature has wisely put round the tender mind. The child even has a natural craving for horrors. He survives just because he is without sentiment, for only in this way can his green heart harden sufficiently to withstand the wounds that wait for it.

The nature writer W H Hudson agrees. His 'green heart' matured at the moment that he first began to realise his own mortality, that is, when he first became part of death's idea, could apply it to himself.

William Hudson was brought up on a farm in Argentina, and as a boy thralled to tales of gouchos revelling in a victim's fearful agonies before – mercifully – cutting his throat. It was hard, savage country.

W H Hudson, growing up in a farm in Argentina in the mid-19th Century, knew more about farm horrors than most: 'The native manner of killing a cow or bullock at that time was peculiarly painful.'

The native manner of killing a cow or bullock at that time was peculiarly painful. Occasionally it would be slaughtered out of sight on the plain, and the hide and flesh brought in by the men, but as a rule, the beast would be driven up close to the house to save trouble. One of the two or three mounted men engaged in the operation would throw his lasso over the horns, and galloping off, pull the rope taut; a second man would then drop from his horse, and running up to the animal behind, pluck out his big knife and with two lightening-quick blows sever the tendons of both hind legs. . . instantly the beast would go down on his haunches, and the same man, knife in hand, would flit round to its front or side, and, watching his opportunity, presently thrust the long blade into its throat just above the chest, driving it into the hilt and working it round; then when it was withdrawn a great torrent of blood would pour out from the tortured beast, still standing on his fore-legs, bellowing all the time with agony. At this point the slaughterer would often leap lightly on its back, stick his spurs in its sides, and, using the flat of his long knife as a whip, pretend to be riding a race, yelling with fiendish glee. The bellowing would subside into deep, awful, sob-like sounds and chokings; then the rider, seeing the animal about to collapse, would fling himself nimbly off. The beast down, they would all run to it, and throwing themselves on its quivering side as on a couch, begin making and lighting cigarettes.

To me it was an awful object-lesson, and held me fascinated with horror. For this was death! The crimson torrents of blood, the deep, human-like cries, made the beast appear like some huge, powerful man caught in a snare by small, weak, but cunning adversaries, who tortured him for their delight and mocked him in his agony.

This, then, was the savage milieu of Hudson's childhood. The horror of death hypnotised him, but didn't touch his heart until after what he describes as 'the most important event of my childhood'. His dog, Caesar, was thirteen and dying slowly and painfully of old age.

No one dreamed of such a thing as putting an end to him – no hint of such a thing was ever spoken. It was not the custom in that country to shoot an old dog because he was past work. I remember his last day, and how often we came back to look at him and tried to comfort him with warm rugs and the offer of food and drink . . . that night he died, we knew it as soon as we were up in the morning. Then, after breakfast, during which we had been very solemn and quiet, our schoolmaster said: 'We must bury him . . .'

When all was done, while we were standing silently around, it came into Mr Trigg's mind to improve the occasion. Assuming his schoolroom expression he looked round at us and said solemnly: 'That's the end. Every dog has his day and so has every man; and the end is the same for both. We die like old Caesar, and are put into the ground and have the earth shovelled over us.'

Now these simple, common words affected me more than any other words I have heard in my life. They pierced me to the heart. I had heard something terrible – too terrible to think of, incredible . . .

I had heard of death – I knew there was such a thing; I knew that all animals had to die, also that some men died. For how could anyone, even a child in its sixth year, overlook such a fact, in a land of battle, murder, and sudden death? I knew that there was good and evil in the world, good and bad men, and the bad men – murderers, thieves, and liars – would all have to die, just like animals. All the others, myself and my own people included, were good and would never taste death . . .

And now these never-to-be-forgotten words spoken over the grave of our old dog had come to awaken me from that beautiful dream of perpetual joy!

When I recall this event I am less astonished at my ignorance than at the intensity of the feeling I experienced, the terrible darkness it brought on so young a mind.

Becoming part of the idea of death, recognising one's own mortality, is a stage the poet, Wordsworth, noted, too.

Nothing was more difficult for me in childhood than the notion of death as a state applicable to my own being. I have said elsewhere,

> A simple child
> That lightly draws its breath
> And feels its life in every limb,
> What should it know of death?

But it was not so much from the source of animal vivacity that my difficulty came as from a sense of the indomitableness of the spirit within me. I used to brood over the stories of Enoch and Elijah, and almost to persuade myself

As Herbert (centre, above left) *grew, he began to look beyond the 'fine simple stony architecture' of the farm: Rievaulx Abbey*

(above) *'played an important part in the growth of my imagination . . . so lovely then in its solitude and desolation.'*

that, whatever might become of others, I should be translated in something of the same way to heaven.

Both Read and the poet, Edwin Muir, believed that a child could not grow up in a better place than a farm, a place where discordant elements coexist without question: life and death, joy and sadness, the real world in which, so Wordworth wrote,

> Tumult and peace, the darkness and the light –
> Were all like workings of one mind, the features
> Of the same face.

But, unlike Muir, it is not the farm with which Read connects the birth of his artistic imagination. The Reads rarely ventured far, perhaps once a year to collect timber on the edge of the moors. But sometimes an expedition was undertaken when Herbert was staying with an aunt (his mother being the youngest in a family of nine, there were plenty to choose from).

One lived in a cottage at Helmsley. Was it from there that he first went to Duncombe Park, and the antique walls of Rievaulx discovered a new dimension to the inscape of the young boy's mind?

Duncombe Park was an amazing wonderland, which we entered but rarely, and always with an awe communicated by our deferential elders. My eyes searched the wide vistas for some limiting hedge, but in vain. We stopped to stroke a newly-born deer. Vanbrugh's mansion was something beyond my comprehension . . . Overhanging a steep valley at the end of the park is a famous terrace, with a lawn as smooth as a carpet and a Grecian temple at each end. Down in this valley is the abbey of Rievaulx.

Rievaulx played an important part in the growth of my imagination, but I cannot tell how much of its beauty and romance was absorbed in these years of childhood, how much built on to these memories in later years. It was the farthest western limit of my wanderings, and so lovely then in its solitude and desolation, that I think my childish mind, in spite of its overwheening objectivity, must have surrendered to its subtle atmosphere. One day, years later, I happened to be there when . . . a choir had come from York Minster, and sang a *Te Deum* between the ruined arches; their sweet voices echoing strangely under the roof of the sky, their white surplices fluttering in the wind. The tomb of Sir Walter l'Espec, the knight who had founded the abbey and had afterwards died as a monk in these cloisters, stood at the end of the chancel. It was not dedicated to any known God, but in a moment of solitude it would serve as an altar to a sense of glory denoted by these ruins and this tomb, and their existence in this solitary place.

BB

b. 1905

'Small children have such vivid imaginations: sounds, colours, weather, even the behaviour and aspect of grown-ups, all fit into private mind pictures.'

In his memoir, 'A Child Alone', the illustrator and author of some fifty books about the English countryside and creatures that inhabit it, Denys Watkins-Pitchford (known as BB to his readers) wonders at the mind's poor selectivity in retaining apparently unimportant moments of childhood in memory.

One of my father's favourite walks, and mine too, was from Galmpton to Greenway Ferry on the Dart. We must have gone by train from Torquay. I always associate the very early days of spring with the road – a lane then – which leads down from Galmpton to the ferry, where one tolled a bell to summon the ferryman who rowed across from the opposite shore. The first primroses starred that little lane and the pale sunlight, shining on the steep banks, lit up the red buds forming on the elm trees.

I have a recollection, too, of returning one late evening to Torquay over a common dotted with gorse bushes, and saw in the distance the lights of Torquay spread out below, and the men-of-war in the harbour. All was calm and still with the light dying over the sea. There was a faint perfume in the air which suggested spring was near.

How very strange it is that quite uneventful moments in life such as this remain so long in memory! It was just that I felt the nearness of spring and

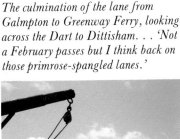

The culmination of the lane from Galmpton to Greenway Ferry, looking across the Dart to Dittisham. . . 'Not a February passes but I think back on those primrose-spangled lanes.'

The Rectory at Lamport. 'We slept in a large airy room on the first floor.' Second window from the left, the room where the last gnome in England made its appearance to BB when four.

the loveliness of being alive . . . not a February passes but I think back on those primrose-spangled lanes.

Was it on the same holiday that BB explored alone, at low tide, the rocky foreshore at Corbyn Head, 'so crystal clear and full of treasures, rose-pink seaweed fronds, crabs, the glutinous sinister jellies of sea anemonies clinging to the rocks, the clean washed sand, and the delicate little shells so finely chased, pearly pink and white, ribbed like fine china? What treasures . . . what magic for a child.'

BB retained the magic of childhood all his life; his precise unsentimental images owe much to the open channels his imagination maintained with those fresh images of beauty and joy – 'the loveliness of being alive' – first imprinted on his mind.

His memories went back almost to the beginning.

When at last we [he and his twin brother, Roger] could walk, I began to take a deeper interest in my surroundings. I remember walking with Nicky [their governess] down to the Post Office in the village, and the print of her pattens which she wore to keep her feet out of the mire.

All little boys delight in mud, and in that far-off time the roads in winter were truly as Shakespeare describes them in winter, 'when ways be foul'. There was special magic in those miry roads – in the soft ridges, like plasticine, neatly patterned by the wheels of passing carts and carriages, and where the road was overhung with trees, the beautiful porridge of mud and leaves which, mingling together, had a most delicious bouquet.

As I must have been only a matter of twenty-four inches or so from this lovely mess, I could relish the smell, feel and sight of it in a very personal way. I liked to study the precise prints of the pram wheels – I don't think bicycles were then in general use – and the half-moon spoor of horses and the hobnailed prints of rustic boots.

This memory dates back to an exciting time when Denys's father, rector of Lamport, a little village deep in the forgotten loveliness of Northamptonshire, purchased a cart and small pony, and Nicky was taught to drive it.

For a while, until one day the pony bolted, it was a highly popular mode of transport for the boys. Probably the emotive context of the memory – Denys's excitement at riding in the cart for the first time – is what fixed the memory fast in mind. His other 'moments' are memorable as part of the happy glow of family holidays.

But the imprinting of patterns on mud throws up an interesting interpretive image of how first sensations imprint ideas on the mind of a child. Sensations – 'the smell, feel and sight of it' – impress themselves upon him 'in a very personal way' – their emotional content, warmth, excitement, intimacy, joy, moulding the contours of the boy's mind like the wheels in the mud, preparing ruts and ridges to guide future thoughts and associations back to the truth at the heart of first-time experience.

First-time sensations have a purity never to be repeated, because never again will they be experienced new, never again will they occur uncompared.

All the 'moments' of BB's childhood experience, far from being 'uneventful', 'strange', seem to call up Wordsworth's concept of the 'dark inscrutable workmanship' of Nature –

> . . . from my first dawn
> Of childhood didst thou intertwine for me
> The passions that build up our human soul.

The focus of remembered childhood images – primroses, light, rock pools, mud – helped cultivate his interest in nature and the countryside, and his reading as a child helped mould the countryman he became:

Bat-fowling: netting a hedgeful of sparrows, finches and thrushes for oyster-cock pie. 'It sounds dreadful in these days of conservation, but I'm told it was very tasty.'

In those late winter evenings, my father read me Richard Jefferies . . . 'Wild Life in a Southern County' was my favourite and I could almost smell the chalk downs.

After Jefferies I discovered W H Hudson. Now here was a writer who really stirred me! Jefferies was a miniature painter; he went from one subject to another in his descriptive prose, but Hudson painted with a broad brush on a big canvas.

Following his tutors, BB's adult vision of nature was primitivist. He was a hunter by nature. When the writer Philip Oakes (whose tale of this introduced me to BB) was a boy of fourteen he wrote to the man to ask him where he might go to shoot geese. BB told him, warning him to be careful as he himself had been blinded in one eye by a blow-back from a shotgun: 'I was trying to pot a blue-tit. Serves me right.' In the course of their acquaintance BB told Oakes about a custom more extraordinary even than shooting blue-tits to the ears of caring souls: bat-fowling. The idea was to net one side of a hedge and beat the other so that sparrows, finches and thrushes, in their effort to escape, snared themselves in the net and became the filling for a dish known as oyster-cock pie. 'It sounds dreadful,' said BB. 'But I'm told it was very tasty.'

BB, then, was a countryman through and through, but a countryman, it soon became apparent, with a vivid imagination that was soon forming its own highly individual and, as it turned out, lucrative, 'ruts and ridges'.

Writing about the old nursery reminds me that my favourite place was by the west window which, like the windows in the drawing-room downstairs, smelled of dead flies.

Sometimes the casement made a little intermittent knocking noise in a wind and this sound, in some curious way, made a deep impression on my imagination. The gentle knocks, always coming when one least expected them, conjured up in my mind strange visions of far away places – ships at sea, golden fields of wavy corn, evening, woods and streams, and of times long gone . . .

Why should this have been? How could the sound of wood knocking on wood affect me in that way? The fact is that small children have such vivid imaginations: sounds, colours, weather, even the behaviour and aspect of grown-ups, all fit into private mind pictures.

My next memory is of rather an unusual nature and the reader will dismiss it out of hand as being mere childhood fancy.

It occurred when we were about four years old.

We slept in the nursery, a large airy room on the first floor, and our beds were side by side with a small space between. It was summer time. The shutters had been closed, but as it was only around six or seven o'clock in the evening it was, of course, still light outside and the room full of daylight.

I can remember I was listening to the sound of a far away warbling blackbird in the lime trees on the drive – a song which still has a delicious airy quality for me. Of all bird songs in Britain it has an exquisite melody, like the rich pure notes of a wind instrument.

Roger was asleep in the next bed but I was far from feeling sleepy. I was busy conjuring up a picture of the sunny garden outside where I could hear the click of croquet balls coming from the lawn . . .

I lay on my right side facing away from the tall windows where the soft evening light gleamed through chinks in the shutters. Something made me turn over, quickly, to face the windows, and there, between the beds was a diminutive Being. It had a round, very red, bearded face about the size of a small crab apple – it had, I think, some sort of hat on its head, but I was never clear about this.

Astonishment was mutual. I was stricken with fright as was the small object which immediately, and with great swiftness, bobbed down between the beds.

I lay for the moment trying to understand what I had just seen and my reaction was one of terror, though why this should be so I don't know as it had been a merry little face and not at all malevolent – quite the reverse. I suppose it was terror of the unknown.

Denys opened his mouth and bawled lustily. Nicky appeared and when he told her that he had just seen a little man, who had disappeared under the bed, she looked, reassured him that nothing was there, and told him it had just been a dream. 'But it wasn't a dream. I can still see the little red astonished face.'

Much later, that gnome – 'the last gnome in England' – made BB into a bestselling author. He borrowed him for his classic story for children, 'The Little Grey Men', replicating him in the persons of Sneezewort, Baldmoney, Dodder & Co who pursue their adventures up the Folly Brook, which runs through the valley just below the Rectory at Lamport.

Of course, these are gnomes coloured richly by BB's country-man persona – 'honest-to-goodness gnomes, none of your baby, fairy-book tinsel stuff, and they live by hunting and fishing, like the animals and birds, which is only proper and right'.

Easter Monday, 1914, was another happy day that spring when we boys followed the brook up from Lamport station almost to its source to the north of Draughton village.

The intimate bends where old oaks leaned, airy shingle spits, gurgling runs where some fallen branch had diverted the main current, how the brook coiled and doubled on itself, its banks lined with bird-sown hawthorns. Silver dace dwelt in this stream and numerous sticklebacks.

It was this stream which, years later, was the inspiration for my Carnegie Medal-winning story 'The Little Grey Men'; it was the memory of that Easter Monday walk which helped colour my story of the three little men (no doubt I had been helped, also, by the vision of the apple-faced gnome which had appeared to me when I lay in bed in the nursery at the Rectory) and how they explored the Folly Brook.

'The intimate bends where old oaks leaned, fairy shingle spits, gurgling runs where some fallen branch had diverted the main current, how the brook coiled and doubled on itself.'

'Many winter floods had laid bare some of the massive hawser roots which projected in a twisted tangle from the soil of the bank. The sun, shining full on the steep bluff, threw shadows from the overhanging roots, so that underneath all was darkness. Something moved in the shadow under the root.

'He came out from under the root very slowly, peeping first one way and then another, listening.' The Little Grey Men

Today, it is all there, just as BB described. The coiling brook and intimate bends, the fairy shingle spits, the fallen boughs diverting the main current. As are many of the descriptions – including the home of the gnomes beneath the roots of an oak – reserved for the novel itself, as my photographs show.

What took me by surprise, was how miniature everything was. I had in mind, from BB's drawings, a brook at least twelve feet across (one drawing has a boy in it who lends it that order of scale), but in fact the brook is tiny. Everything is of elfin proportion. Of course BB was writing his story through the eyes of the boy on that Easter Monday ramble. It wouldn't have seemed tiny to him.

Edwin Muir

b. 1887

***'A child could not grow up in a better place than a farm . . . A
farm is such a carnival of birth and death.'***

Son of a tenant farmer, the poet Edwin Muir spent his childhood
in Orkney, moving at fourteen to Glasgow. Much of the imagery of
his poetry is rooted in his childhood landscape. 'The little island
was not too big for a child to see in it an image of life,' he records in
his 'Autobiography': 'land and sea and sky, good and evil,
happiness and grief, life and death discovered themselves to me
there; and the landscape was so simple that it made these things
simple too.'

Particular childhood 'clips' of the island appear in his poetry,
too, as when watching his father sowing grain, Edwin catches a
ship passing 'so slowly against the black hills that it seemed to be
stationary, though when my attention returned to it again I saw
with wonder that it had moved.' The poem captures the still,
quiet, timeless island landscape well.

Long time he lay upon the sunny hill
To his father's house below securely bound.
Far off the silent, changing sound was still,
With the black islands lying thick around.

He saw each separate height, each vaguer hue,
Where the massed islands rolled in mist away,
And though all ran together in his view
He knew that unseen straits between them lay.

Often he wondered what new shores were there.
In thought he saw the still light on the sand,
The shallow water clear in tranquil air,
And walked through it in joy from strand to strand.

Over the sound a ship so slow would pass
That in the black hill's gloom it seemed to lie.
The evening sound was smooth like sunken glass,
And time seemed finished ere the ship passed by.

Grey tiny rocks slept round him where he lay,
Moveless as they, more still as evening came,
The grasses threw straight shadows far away,
And from the house his mother called his name.

'Childhood'

The Bu on Wyre where Edwin spent his early childhood.

When I try to find out what it was that influenced me, I can only think of the years of childhood which I spent on my father's farm in the little island of Wyre in Orkney, and the beauty I apprehended then, before I knew there was beauty.

These years had come alive, after being forgotten for so long and when I wrote about horses they were my father's plough-horses as I saw them when I was four or five, and a poem on Achilles pursuing Hector round the walls of Troy was really a resuscitation of the afternoon when I ran away, in real terror, from another boy when I returned from school. The bare landscape of the little island became, without my knowing it, a universal landscape over which Abraham and Moses and Achilles and Ulysses and Tristram and all sorts of pilgrims passed; and Troy was associated with the Castle, a mere green mound, near my father's house.

All at once I saw a blue sailor's suit with a yellow twisted hempen cord loosely knotted round the collar; and at the end of it a canary-yellow wooden whistle. The sailor suit startled me so much that I did not know what to do with it. Next moment I realised that I had worn it once; I could remember distinctly the feel and the smell of the smooth wooden whistle; it had a faint fragrant smell. . . It must have been one of the things I loved most as a child, since even in memory I could feel the delight it had given me.

I can still see the sailor suit; I can see the rough grey stones spotted with lichen on the top of the Castle, and a bedraggled gooseberry bush in a corner of the garden whose branches I lovingly fingered for hours; but I cannot bring back the feelings which I had for them, the sense of being magically close to them, as if they were magnets drawing me with a palpable power. Reasonable explanations can be found for these feelings: the fact that every object is new to a child, that he sees it without understanding it or understands it without a different understanding from that of experience – different, for there may be fear in it, but there cannot be calculation or worry; or even the fact that he is closer to things since his eyes are only two or three feet from the ground, not five or six. Grass, stones, and insects are twice as near to him as they will be after he has grown up, and when I try to re-create my early childhood it seems to me that it was focused on such things as these, and that I lived my life in a small, separate underworld, while the grown-ups walked on their long legs several feet above my head on a stage where every relation was different. I was dizzily lifted into that world, as into another dimension, when my father took me on his shoulders, so that I could see the roof of the byre from above or touch the lintel of the house door with my hand. But for most of the time I lived with whatever I found on the surface of the earth: the different kinds of grass, the daisies, buttercups, dandelions, bog cotton (we did not have many flowers), the stones and bits of glass and china, and the scurrying insects which made my stomach heave as I stared at them, unable to take my eyes away.

These insects were all characters to me, interesting but squalid, with thoughts that could never be penetrated, inconceivable aims, perverse activities. I knew their names, which so exactly fitted them as characters: the Jenny Hunderlegs, the gavelock, the forkytail, the slater – the underworld of my little underworld, obsessing me, but for ever beyond my reach. Some were not so horrible, such as the spider, impersonal compared with the others, whose progress was a terrifying dart or a grave, judge-like, swaying walk. Unlike the others he was at home in the sun, and so did not need to scuttle; I thought of him as bearded and magistral. I could never bear to touch any of these creatures, though I watched them so closely that I seemed to be taking part in their life, which was like little fragments of night darting about in the sun; they often came into my dreams later, wakening me in terror. How many hours I must have spent staring with fixed loathing at these creatures! Yet I did not want to know anything about them; I merely wanted them away. Their presence troubled me as the mind is troubled in adolescence by the realisation of physical lust. The gavelocks and forkytails were my first intimation of evil, and associations of evil still cling round them for me, as, I fancy, for most people: popular imagery shows it. We cannot tell how much our minds are influenced for life by the fact that we see the world first at a range of two or three feet.

The insects, of course, were only a small part of that three-foot world; I think I must have passed through a phase of possession by them, comparatively short. The grass was a reliable pleasure; the flowers were less dependable, and after I picked a dandelion one day and found it writhing with little angry, many-legged insects, the faces of the flowers took on a faithless look, until my mother taught me which could be relied upon. The crevices in stone walls were filled with secrets; a slab of hard cement on the wall of the house had a special meaning. Mud after new rain was delicious, and I was charmed by everything that flew, from the humble bee to the Willie Longlegs. At that stage the novelty of seeing a creature flying outweighed everything else.

My height from the ground determined my response to other things too.

'When my father and Sutherland brought in the horses from the fields I stood trembling among their legs . . . looking up at the stationary hulks and the tossing heads, which in the winter dusk were lost in the sky.'

When my father and Sutherland brought in the horses from the fields I stood trembling among their legs, seeing only their great, bearded feet and the momentary flash of their crescent-shaped shoes flung up lazily as they passed. When my father stopped with the bridle in his hands to speak to me I stood looking up at the stationary hulks and the tossing heads, which in the winter dusk were lost in the sky. I felt beaten down by an enormous weight and a real terror; yet I did not hate the horses as I hated the insects; my fear turned into something else, for it was infused by a longing to go up to them and touch them and simultaneously checked by the knowledge that their hoofs were dangerous: a combination which added up to worship in the Old Testament sense. Everything about them, the steam rising from their soft, leathery nostrils, the sweat staining their hides, their ponderous, irresistible motion, the distant rolling of their eyes, which was like the revolution of rock-crystal suns, the waterfall sweep of their manes, the ruthless flick of their cropped tails, the plunge of their iron-shod hoofs striking fire from the flagstones, filled me with a stationery terror and delight for which I could get no relief. One day two of our horses began to fight in the field below the house rearing at each other like steeds on a shield and flinging out with their hind-legs, until Sutherland rushed out to separate them. A son of our neighbour at the Haa had a crescent mark on his forehead where a horse had kicked him; I stared at it in entrancement, as if it were a sign from the sky. And in a copy of 'Gulliver's Travels' which my eldest brother had won as a school prize there was a picture of a great horse sitting on a throne judging a crowd of naked men with hairy hangdog faces. The horse was sitting on its hindquarters, which had a somewhat mean and inadequate appearance; its front hoofs were upraised and its neck arched as if to strike; and though the picture was strange and frightening, I took it to be the record of some actual occurrence. All this added to my terror of horses, so that I loved and dreaded them as an explorer loves and dreads a strange country which he has not yet entered.

Edwin Muir perceives 'zones of childhood' through which we pass before entering that 'strange country'. The very young child exists in a state near to immortality because he is oblivious to time: 'Time does not exist for us. We pay no attention to time until he tugs us by the sleeve or claps his policeman's hand on our shoulder; it is in our nature to ignore him, but he will not be ignored.' This is the phase that Herbert Read called the 'innocent years . . . in which we seemed not so much to live as to be lived by forces outside us.'

The very young child perceives a completer harmony of all things with each other than he will ever know again. 'I think of this picture or vision as that of a state in which the earth, the houses on the earth, and the life of every human being are related to the sky overarching them; as if the sky fitted the earth and the earth the sky.'

'There comes a moment (the moment at which childhood passes into boyhood or girlhood) when this image is broken and contradiction enters life. It is a phase of emotional and mental strain, and it brings with it a sense of guilt.'

This progress (or retreat perhaps) from instinctual harmony to contradiction and guilt, is unavoidable, written on man's collective sub-conscious since the dawn of time.

His instinctual sense of harmony harks back to an Age when it was used, for example, to effect a special mutual understanding between man and animals. He sees this era depicted in myth and ancient reliefs – a fabulous Age of heraldic men and legendary beasts.

'The age which felt this connection between men and animals was so much longer than the brief historical period known to us that we cannot conceive it; but our subconscious life goes back into it.'

It was a relationship that seems nonetheless to have allowed the hunting instinct of man and animal to subsist. 'Some of the animals were sacred and some monstrous, some quaint and ugly as house gods; they were worshipped and sacrificed; they were hunted; and the hunt, like the worship and the sacrifice, was a ritual act . . . Man felt guilty towards them, for he took their lives day after day, in obedience to a custom so long established that no one could say when it began. Though he killed them, they were sacred to him, because without destroying them he could not live. As their life had to be taken and the guilt for it accepted, the way of taking it was important, and the ritual [sacrifice] arose, to which were united the ideas of necessity and guilt, turning the killing into a mystery . . . ' Thus did the contradiction and guilt emerge in man's psyche, and he assuage it.

Now, today, we have sanitised our relationship with animals. We kill them in their thousands in slaughterhouses, out of the way, out of sight, out of conscience.

We no longer feel the guilt and no longer assuage it because we no longer have the special understanding. We have lost the faculty capable of such an intuitional understanding, a primitive 'animism', that is a faculty of earliest childhood.

Muir seems to be looking for a grand parallel between phases in childhood and changes that man has undergone in the process of civilisation. In religious terms, though he doesn't restrict his convictions to mythologies as recent as Christianity, the process is from innocence (the Garden of Eden) through guilt (recognising sin) and on, either to discovering a purpose in the dream or closing our eyes to it altogether.

For many of the writers in this book the final zone of childhood would be the awakening of a creative imagination that fulfils the purpose of childhood, Herbert Read's 'sense of glory', or Wordsworth's 'auxiliary light . . . which in the setting sun/ Bestowed new splendour', and which the poet links inextricably to childhood experience, 'the fountain light of all our day . . . a master light of all our seeing'.

William Wordsworth

b. 1770

*'The mind of man is fashioned and built up
Even as a strain of music . . . '*

Wordsworth's 'The Prelude' is his autobiography. The passages about his childhood are unique among records of rural childhood experience because they offer often stunningly immediate and evocative recreations of childhood events within an inspired explanation of how the events moulded the mind of a true poet.

Dove Cottage at Grasmere, Wordsworth's home where most of 'The Prelude' was written.

William's great gift to us was to restore man's contact with the primitive, to refresh man's intuitive powers wasted away by centuries of pomposity and Reason. He took us back to an earlier time (which we may recognise because it is, in effect, the time of childhood) when man and nature were one. The child fresh out of nature's womb does not distinguish himself from nature, does not see himself as separate; his soul still resounds to echoes of the music of the celestial spheres. Only subdued by 'the regular action of the world' does the adult resort to the scientific apparatus of Reason to disentangle the unholy, man-made mess.

There is a moral purpose, too, in the story of this orphaned boy, for whom the craggy fells and soft green valleys of Cumbria became, respectively, stern mentor and nurse. In 'Tintern Abbey' he is –

> . . . well pleased to recognise
> In nature and the language of the sense
> The anchor of my purest thoughts, the nurse,
> The guide, the guardian of my heart, and soul
> Of all my moral being.

– and in his autobiography he shows us how nature performed this miraculous course.

William was born in Cockermouth on April 7th, 1770, the second of five children. His father was an attorney who became estate manager to Sir James Lowther, the principal landlord in the Lake District.

The River Derwent flowed past his house, and it is the main memory of his earliest days that –

> . . . the fairest of all rivers, loved
> To blend his murmurs with my nurse's song,
> And, from his alder shades and rocky falls,
> And from his fords and shallows, sent a voice
> That flowed along my dreams . . .

> giving me
> Amid the fretful dwellings of mankind
> A foretaste, a dim earnest, of the calm
> That Nature breathes among the hills and groves.

His first seven years in the bosom of his family are remembered as idyllic, all seemingly summer, long days spent bathing in the river, basking in the sun, or coursing over the fields and leaping through 'groves of yellow groundsel', or just standing alone . . .

> Beneath the sky, as if I had been born
> On Indian plains, and from my mother's hut
> Had run abroad in wantonness, to sport
> A naked savage, in the thunder shower.

Then, in 1778, tragedy strikes. While on holiday with his mother (Ann Cookson) and his three brothers – Richard, John and Christopher – and sister, Dorothy, at their grandfather's house in Penrith, Ann dies. She is only thirty-one.

Extraordinarily, the children stay on in Penrith rather than being returned to their father in Cockermouth. To her horror, Dorothy (only seven years old) is separated from her brothers and dispatched to live with Ann's cousin in Halifax and the following year, Richard and William are sent to Hawkshead Grammar School in the Vale of Esthwaite, where they are lodged with a kind couple called Hugh and Anne Tyson.

It is difficult to imagine the grief and anguish that the children must have suffered at this turn of events – losing their mother, being split up (William and Dorothy were especially close, she being just one year younger than him), to all intents losing a father, too, and being shipped off to places which, however lovely, they didn't know as home. Yet thus did William become, effectively, an orphan.

The interior of Hawkshead School, where William was educated from 1779 to 1787, a time when he received so many of the impressions that inspired his work.

Without father or mother, he gives himself to the sun and moon:

> Daily the common range of visible things
> Grew dear to me: already I began
> To love the sun; a boy I loved the sun,
> Not as I since have loved him, as a pledge
> And surety of our earthly life, a light
> Which we behold and feel we are alive;
> Not for his bounty to so many worlds –
> But for this cause, that I had seen him lay
> His beauty on the morning hills, had seen
> The western mountain touch his setting orb,
> In many a thoughtless hour, when, from excess
> Of happiness, my blood appeared to flow
> For its *own* pleasure, and I breathed with joy.
> And, from like feelings, humble though intense,
> To patriotic and domestic love
> Analagous, the moon to me was dear;
> For I would dream away my purposes,

Esthwaite, 'thou one dear Vale'.

> Standing to gaze upon her while she hung
> Midway between the hills, as if she knew
> No other region, but belonged to thee,
> Yea, appertained by a peculiar right
> To thee and thy grey huts, thou one dear Vale!

Four years later, when William is at home for the Christmas holidays, the family cord is cut completely. His father dies. For William it is the final stroke. 'The event, With all the sorrow that it brought, appeared a chastisement.' He turns to God for forgiveness, and he receives, as it were in response, an image in memory of a scene he had witnessed ten days earlier while waiting to be picked up after school and taken home for the fateful holiday:

> One Christmas-time,
> On the glad eve of its dear holidays,
> Feverish, and tired, and restless, I went forth
> Into the fields, impatient for the sight
> Of those led palfreys that should bear us home;
> My brothers and myself. There rose a crag,
> That, from the meeting-point of two highways
> Ascending, overlooked them both, far stretched;
> Thither, uncertain on which road to fix
> My expectation, thither I repaired,
> Scout-like, and gained the summit; 'twas a day
> Tempestuous, dark, and wild, and on the grass
> I sate half-sheltered by a naked wall;
> Upon my right hand couched a single sheep,
> Upon my left a blasted hawthorn stood . . .

'. . .'Twas a day/Tempestuous, dark, and wild,

. . .Upon my left a blasted hawthorn stood'

The scene comes back to him not simply as a visual frame but as an insight, a revelation that cauterises the emotional wound – an image, perhaps, of nature as harbinger of both life *and* death – and relieves the boy of his sense of guilt.

> And, afterwards, the wind and sleety rain,
> And all the business of the elements,
> The single sheep, and the one blasted tree,
> And the bleak music of that old stone wall,
> The noise of wood and water, and the mist
> That on the line of each of those two roads
> Advanced in such indisputable shapes;
> All these were kindred spectacles and sounds
> To which I oft repaired, and thence would drink,
> As at a fountain.

Wordsworth catalogues the experience in 'The Prelude' among moments of profound significance:

> There are in our existence spots of time,
> That with distinct pre-eminence retain
> A renovating virtue, whence, depressed . . .
>   our minds
> Are nourished and invisibly repaired.

Back in school, he and his friends throw themselves into play as determinedly as the excellent Grammar school at Hawkshead establishes a scholarly rapport –

> We were a noisy crew; the sun in heaven
> Beheld not vales more beautiful than ours;
> Nor saw a band in happiness and joy
> Richer, or worthier of the ground they trod.

Fishing in mountain brooks; rowing on Lake Windermere; riding out on horseback to 'some famed temple where of yore The Druids worshipped,' or riding the twenty-one miles to 'the antique walls Of that large Abbey' (Furness Abbey); playing bowls on the 'smooth platform' of the green of The White Lion, Bowness, where 'bursts of glee Made all the mountains ring'; bird's nesting high up on the Yewdale crags; and skating on frozen Windermere in winter –

>   . . . for me
> It was a time of rapture! Clear and loud
> The village clock tolled six, – I wheeled about,
> Proud and exulting like an untired horse
> That cares not for his home. All shod with steel,
> We hissed along the polished ice in games

Skating on Windermere (taken on Feb. 17th, 1929). 'All shod with steel,/We hissed along the polished ice'.

Confederate, imitative of the chase
And woodland pleasures, – the resounding horn,
The pack loud chiming, and the hunted hare. . .

Not seldom from the uproar I retired
Into a silent bay, or sportively
Glanced sideway, leaving the tumultuous throng,
To cut across the reflex of a star
That fled, and, flying still before me, gleamed
Upon the glassy plain; and oftentimes,
When we had given our bodies to the wind,
And all the shadowy banks on either side
Came sweeping through the darkness, spinning still
The rapid line of motion, then at once
Have I, reclining back upon my heels,
Stopped short; yet still the solitary cliffs
Wheeled by me – even as if the earth had rolled
With visible motion her diurnal round!
Behind me they did stretch in solemn train,
Feebler and feebler, and I stood and watched
Till all was tranquil as a dreamless sleep.

Looking back, the adult poet perceives nature's purpose – a teaching purpose, both moral and aesthetic – in these 'boyish sports'. Fishing: the rod and line may be 'True symbol of the

Hawkshead village – 'I saw the snow-white church upon the hill / Sit like a throned lady'. That is how Wordsworth pictured it when he wrote of his return to the village after his first year at Cambridge University in 1788. Three years earlier it had been roughcast afresh by two local wallers, and its 'snow-white' cladding was not removed until 1875-6. Nevertheless, the church remains a distinctive feature of the view for miles around. T W Thompson, author of the Hawkshead Church booklet (first edition 1956) has it from local sources – William himself told one Miss Mary Hodgson of Green End, Hawkshead, that as a boy he'd often walk up to the churchyard on summer evenings and look out over the Vale. There's still a long stone bench attached to the east wall, and Hawkshead folk will still tell you that Church End, as it is called, commands the best view.

foolishness of hope' (none other than a boy angler could have coined that line), but it leads him to out-of-the-way mountain spots of rare beauty, to rocks and pools 'shut out from every star', to 'forlorn cascades Among the windings hid of mountain brooks'.

Competitive rowing on lake Windermere finds conquered and conqueror resting on their oars side-by-side near some 'Island musical with birds That sang and ceased not'.

> Thus the pride of strength,
> And the vain-glory of superior skill,
> Were tempered; thus was gradually produced
> A quiet independence of the heart'.

At ruined Furness Abbey, as 'With whip and spur we through the chantry flew In uncouth race, and left the cross-legged knight, And the stone-abbot', the boisterous scene is suddenly stilled by the voice of a single wren that roots William to the spot in awe.

Even playing bowls at the White Hart inn at Bowness offers a special beauty when, on their return to Hawkshead across Lake Windermere, the boys hear a minstrel blow his flute –

> Alone upon the rock – oh, then, the calm
> And dead still water lay upon my mind
> Even with a weight of pleasure, and the sky,
> Never before so beautiful, sank down
> Into my heart, and held me like a dream!

Caves, trees, woods and hills impress upon the boy ideas of triumph and delight, by means of sensations of hope, danger, and fear, as

> . . . when I have hung
> Above the raven's nest, by knots of grass
> And half-inch fissures in the slippery rock
> But ill sustained, and almost (so it seemed)
> Suspended by the blast which blew amain,
> Shouldering the naked crag, oh, at that time
> While on the perilous ridge I hung alone,
> With what strange utterance did the loud dry wind
> Blow through my ear! the sky seemed not a sky
> Of earth – and with what motion moved the clouds!

Again, when stealing a boat from its willow tree berth on the shores of Patterdale by Ullswater, a rocky moutainous area beyond the impressive Kirkstone Pass from Hawkshead (quite

'. . . when I have hung/Above the raven's nest. . .' Bird's nesting was a favourite hobby of William and his friends at Hawkshead school. In the late spring of 1782, he, together with John Benson, Fletcher and William Raincock, Edward Birkett, and William Tyson made an attempt (with the help of a waller, Tom Usher, whom the boys had wisely asked to accompany them) to get the eggs from a raven's nest on a narrow ledge high up on the Yewdale crags. John Benson froze and became cragfast, and eventually had to be rescued.

High up on the mist-enveloped Kirkstone Pass which takes the traveller from the soft green Vale of Esthwaite, where William resided as a schoolboy, to the rocky shores of Patterdale by Ullswater, where his moral education began.

different to the soft pastoral serenity of Esthwaite Vale), William is taught a moral lesson never to be forgotten:

> I dipped my oars into the silent lake,
> And, as I rose upon the stroke, my boat
> Went heaving through the water like a swan;
> When, from behind that craggy steep till then
> The horizon's bound, a huge peak, black and huge,

As if with voluntary power instinct
Upreared its head. I struck and struck again,
And growing still in stature the grim shape
Towered up between me and the stars, and still,
For so it seemed, with purpose of its own
And measured motion like a living thing,
Strode after me. With trembling oars I turned,
And through the silent water stole my way
Back to the covert of the willow tree;
There in her mooring-place I left my bark, –
And through the meadows homeward went, in grave
And serious mood; but after I had seen
That spectacle, for many days, my brain
Worked with a dim and undetermined sense
Of unknown modes of being; o'er my thoughts
There hung a darkness, call it solitude
Or blank desertion. No familiar shapes
Remained, no pleasant images of trees
Of sea or sky, no colours of green fields;
But huge and mighty forms, that do not live

Ullswater, where William steals a
boat and is terrified into returning it.

> Like living men, moved slowly through the mind
> By day, and were a trouble to my dreams.

William describes the process of his education, thus:

> The mind of man is fashioned and built up
> Even as a strain of music: I believe
> That there are spirits, which, when they would form
> A favoured being, from his very dawn
> Of infancy do open out the clouds
> As at the touch of lightning, seeking him
> With gentle visitation; quiet Powers!

But, as he and his intellect and imagination grow, he begins to notice a change in the way nature affects him.

> Those incidental charms which first attached
> My heart to rural objects, day by day
> Grew weaker.

Nature, hitherto enjoyed as a by-product of sporting or leisure pursuits, often undertaken in a gang of friends, 'now at length was sought For her own sake . . . The mind lay open to a more exact And close communion.' The pupil-teacher relationship matures, and he becomes an active, inspired, more solitary participant –

> An auxiliary light
> Came from my mind, which on the setting sun
> Bestowed new splendour. . .
>   and the midnight storm
> Grew darker in the presence of my eye.

The sun and moon of earlier years undergo a transformation. He cannot recall exactly when this first happened – 'who shall parcel out His intellect by geometric rules, Split like a province into round and square? Who knows the individual hour in which His habits were first sown, even as a seed?' – but now William begins actively to pursue his Muse, 'that universal power', in 'gloom and tumult' no less than in 'tranquil scenes'.

> My morning walks
> Were early; – oft before the hours of school
> I travelled round our little lake, five miles
> Of pleasant wandering . . .
>   when the Vale,
> Yet slumbering, lay in utter solitude.
> How shall I seek the origin? where find

Faith in the marvellous things which then I felt?
Oft in these moments such a holy calm
Would overspread my soul, that bodily eyes
Were utterly forgotten, and what I saw
Appeared like something in myself, a dream,
A prospect in the mind.

Esthwaite Water: '. . . oft before the hours of school/I travelled round our little lake, five miles/Of pleasant wandering. . .'

What lies behind the 'auxiliary light' that William describes coming from his mind, 'which on the setting sun Bestowed new splendour'? What was it in the young poet's mind that made the midnight storm grow 'darker in the presence of my eye'? He cannot be sure, but

. . . let this
Be not forgotten, that I still retained
My first creative sensibility;
That by the regular action of the world
My soul was unsubdued.

The child lived on.

Chapter Three: *The Spirit of Pan*

Heaven lies about us in our infancy!
Shades of the prison-house begin to close
Upon the growing Boy,
But He
Beholds the light, and whence it flows,
He sees it in his joy.
William Wordsworth

Thomas Traherne

b. 1636

'How like an angel came I down!
I nothing in the world did know,
But 'twas Divine.'

Thomas Traherne was born in 1636, the son of a shoemaker from Herefordshire. He went to Hereford Grammar School, founded by Bishop Gilbert in 1636, and, with the help of some patron or relations better-off than his father, the necessary fees were found to pay for him to go to Brasenose College, Oxford. He received his BA in 1656, MA in 1661, and Bachelor of Divinity in 1669.

Traherne's 'Centuries', which contain the first replication of childhood experience in the English language, along with some of his poems, written together in a notebook, were picked up for a few pence on a London bookstall in 1896.

Thomas was a bright and inspired child. He believed – not unlike Wordsworth after him – that adulthood is a process of disinformation, a gradual diminution of intuition, of the capacity to divine truth. Truth was important to Thomas. His recollection of childhood experience should not be thought to have been idealised in the telling. This is – we are assured – how it was. Should you for a moment doubt its veracity, do yourself a service, suspend disbelief for a short while and let a child speak to you across three-and-a-half centuries. Thomas believed – it was his first principle after belief in God – that children should teach the teachers, so that they might unlearn.

All appeared new and strange at first, inexpressibly rare and delightful and beautiful. I was a little stranger which at my entrance into the world was saluted and surrounded with innumerable joys. My knowledge was Divine; I knew by intuition those things which since my apostacy I collected again by the highest reason. My very ignorance was advantageous. I seemed as one brought into the estate of innocence. All things were spotless and pure and glorious . . . I knew not that there were any sins, or complaints, or laws. I dreamed not of poverties, contentions, or vices. All tears and quarrels were hidden from mine eyes. Everything was at rest, free and immortal. I knew nothing of sickness or death or exaction. In the absence of these I was entertained like an angel with the works of God in their splendour and glory; I saw all in the peace of Eden; heaven and earth did sing my Creator's praises, and could not make more melody to Adam than to me. All Time was Eternity, and a perpetual Sabbath. Is it not strange that an infant should be heir to the whole world, and see those mysteries which the books of the learned never unfold?

The corn was orient and immortal wheat which never should be reaped nor was ever sown. I thought it had stood from everlasting to everlasting. The dust and stones of the street were as precious as gold: the gates were at first the end of the world. The green trees when I saw them first through one of the gates transported and ravished me; their sweetness and unusual beauty made my heart to leap, and almost mad with ecstacy, they were such strange and wonderful things . . . Eternity was manifest in the Light of the Day, and something infinite beyond everything appeared, which talked with my expectation and moved my desire.

The City seemed to stand in Eden or to be built in Heaven. The streets were mine, the temple was mine, the people were mine, their clothes and gold and silver were mine, as much as their sparkling eyes, fair skins, and ruddy faces. The skies were mine, and so were the sun and moon and stars, and all the world was mine; and I the only spectator and enjoyer of it. I knew no churlish proprieties, nor bounds, nor divisions; but all properties and divisions were mine, all treasures and the possessors of them.

It was a difficult matter to persuade me that the tinseled ware upon a hobby horse was a fine thing. They did impose upon me and obtrude their gifts that made me believe a ribben or a feather curious. I could not see where was the curiousness or fineness. And to teach me that a purse of gold was at any value seemed impossible, the art by which it becomes so, and the reasons for which it is accounted so were so deep and hidden to my inexperience. So that [human] nature is still nearest to natural things, and farthest off from preternatural . . .

So I began among my playfellows to prize a drum, a fine coat, a penny, a gilded book, etc, who before never dreamed of any such wealth . . . As for the Heavens and Sun and Stars they disappeared, and were no more unto me than the bare walls. So that the strange riches of man's inventions quite overcame the riches of nature . . .

So . . . with much ado I was corrupted, and made to learn the dirty devices of this world, which now I unlearn, and become, as it were, a little child again that I may enter into the Kingdom of God.

Kenneth Grahame

b. 1859

'Then, in that utter clearness of the imminent dawn, while Nature, flushed with fullness of incredible colour, seemed to hold her breath for the event, he looked in the very eyes of the Friend and Helper . . .'

Kenneth Grahame's first-love: 'the cool and secluded reaches of the stripling Thames, remote and dragon-fly haunted.'

For almost the whole of his life, Kenneth Grahame's first-love was 'the cool and secluded reaches of the Thames, the stripling Thames, remote and dragon-fly haunted, before it attained the noise, ribbons and flannels of Folly Bridge,' in short, that section

(All the photographs illustrating Grahame's story were taken by his near contemporary Henry Taunt, and are dated in the 1880s.)

of the river between Streatley and Goring in the west, to Cranbourne and Windsor Castle in the east.

Kenneth first came to it, in sadness, from Edinburgh, a boy of nearly five grieving for his mother who had just died from scarlet fever and for his father who, broken-hearted, had fled abroad to

live by himself. Kenneth, his two elder siblings – Helen and Willie – and Roland, the youngest, were taken in by their grandmother at a large house called The Mount, situated on the banks of the stripling Thames at Cookham Dene.

Henceforth Kenneth's happiest childhood days would be spent playing about on the river, sometimes messing about in boats though more often on foot, so that he came to know the life of the river banks intimately. At first it was a new and unusual world to this city boy, whose knowledge of meadows and rivers was as limited as if he had spent his whole life underground:

It all seemed too good to be true. Hither and thither through the meadows he rambled busily, along the hedgerows, across the copses, finding everywhere birds building, flowers budding, leaves thrusting – everything happy, and productive, and occupied . . . He thought his happiness was complete when, as he meandered aimlessly along, suddenly he stood by the edge of a full-fed river. Never in his life had he seen a river before – this sleek, sinuous, full-bodied animal, chasing and chuckling, gripping things with a gurgle and leaving them with a laugh, to fling itself on fresh playmates that shook themselves free, and were caught and held again. All was a-shake and a-shiver – glints and gleams and sparkles, rustle and swirl, chatter and

'So – this – is – a – River!'

'THE River,' corrected the Rat.

'And you really live by the river? What a jolly life!'

'By it and with it and on it and in it,' said the Rat. 'It's brother and sister to me, and aunts, and company, and food and drink, and (naturally) washing. It's my world and I don't want any other.' The Wind in the Willows

Looking towards Mapledurham House, likely model for Toad Hall and open to the public, from the direction of the 'foamy tumble of a weir'.

bubble. The Mole was bewitched, entranced, fascinated.

But, like Mole, Kenneth began to miss his home, and longed for his mother. The sudden disintegration of his family had taken Kenneth's sensitive soul quite unawares. On the face of it life seemed good: he had the camaraderie of his brothers and sisters, he loved the expeditions and adventures and secret haunts they made as children; there was, too, the awakening of his interest in boats ('there is nothing – absolutely nothing – half so much doing as simply messing around in boats'), and the love that every country child has for long summer days and the woods under winter snow. Young Kenneth joined in all the fun that was on offer down at Cookham Dene and later at Cranbourne, where the Grahames moved with their Grandma in 1866, when the leaking roof at the Mount was declared dangerous. But he always kept something back.

'While he was still young,' his biographer Eleanor Grahame said of him, 'he came to think of himself as someone "who goes alone" . . . For consolation he looked inside himself and began to make up stories, to daydream . . .'

Many commentators have spoken of literary creativity arising from some terrible loss in an author's life. Few can have experienced so savage a wrench as Grahame. His father had been a 'witty and popular advocate' who had risen to become Sheriff-Substitute of Argyllshire before tragedy hit the family. What nature of heart-break was it that this man could dump his four children, all under ten, and flee the country?

Whatever it was, as a result, Kenneth found the need to daydream, and many of his dreams are re-created in 'The Wind in the Willows'.

At thirteen Grahame went to St Edward's School, built near the river just outside Oxford. Here his relationship with the Thames developed ever more deeply, as indeed did his love for the 'good grey gothic'. He felt at home in the peaceful academic atmosphere of the Oxford colleges and couldn't believe it when he was told (on the instructions from afar of his father) that he was not to be allowed to try for University. Instead he went straight into a clerkship in the Bank of England. As ever, Grahame accepted his lot, and consoled himself by taking a house near the Thames in Chelsea, catching a riverboat every day to his office in the City, and at week-ends, taking off for the willow-fringed reaches of the stripling Thames of his early years.

We are told that he worked 'gravely and conscientiously' at the bank – so much so that he rose to attain one of the three highest offices in it, he became Secretary of the Bank of England. The hours were good, however, and allowed him plenty of time to visit his adopted home, often staying at Streatley or Pangbourne, if not at Cookham Dene itself. How far working in the bank went against the grain can be seen from so much of Grahame's work – not least the character of Toad, whose one desire is to escape dreary day-to-day life and find adventure. Indeed one of Grahame's first essays tells the story of a City man who suddenly ups from his office one day, buys a cart in the nearby market and transports himself to the country, to be met with years later on the Ridgeway surrounded by all the paraphernalia of an artist and smoking a pipe.

'The Wind in the Willows' itself was not at first intended by Grahame for publication, being based largely on bedtime stories he began telling his only child, Alistair (known as Mouse), one night when he should have been accompanying his wife to a dinner party. The tale continued in walks and in boats on the river and in letters to his son when he was away in his beloved Fowey, in Cornwall ('the little grey sea town' that the sea-rat in 'Wind in the Willows' knew so well).

Grahame married, late in life, one Eleanor Thomson, who had a

Streatley village. This was one of Kenneth's favourite centres for exploration down river on weekend respites from the Bank of England, and remains ideal for the purpose today.

reputation for being something of an eccentric. When Mouse was six the family returned to live in Cookham Dene, and once back in the cradle of his childhood Grahame discovered that he could 'remember everything I felt then. The part of my brain I used from four till about seven can never have altered. Coming back here awakens every recollection.'

What was it that continuously beckoned Grahame to this riverscape during his life? This part of the Thames was what lit his life as child and man – 'What it hasn't got is not worth having,

Pangbourne village, where Kenneth finally retired and lived in seclusion after the death of his only son, Alistair.

and what it doesn't know is not worth knowing,' says Rat. It was all that was real to him in a life beset with un-real events (Mouse, too, died early, in an accident on a railway line while at Oxford).

To begin with the Thames had been a sort of consolation; wrenched from his own family he had found comfort here, but as child became adolescent he had begun to soak in the magic of the 'remote and dragon-fly' haunted reaches where his stories began to take shape. The riverscape became Kenneth's *spiritual* home, and what he saw at the core of its beauty, what first beckoned him as a young boy who 'had lost what he could hardly be said to have found', he gives to Mole and Rat to discover in 'The Piper at the Gates of Dawn', as they go in search of Little Portly, a foolish otter cub who has gone missing:

The line of the horizon was clear and hard against the sky, and in one particular quarter it showed black against a silvery climbing phosphorescence that grew and grew. At last, over the rim of the waiting earth the moon lifted with slow majesty till it swung clear of the horizon and rode off, free of moorings; and once more they began to see surfaces – meadows widespread, and quiet gardens, and the river itself, from bank to bank, all softly disclosed, all washed clean of mystery and terror, all radiant again as by day, but with a difference that was tremendous. Their old haunts greeted them again in other raiment, as if they had slipped away and put on this pure new apparel and come quietly back, smiling as they shyly waited to see if they would be recognised again under it.

Fastening their boat to a willow, the friends landed in this silent, silver kingdom, and patiently explored the hedges, the hollow trees, the runnels and their little culverts, the ditches and dry water-ways. Embarking again and crossing over, they worked their way up the stream in this manner, while the moon, serene and detatched in a cloudless sky, did what she could, though so far off, to help them in their quest; till her hour came and she sank earthwards reluctantly, and left them, and mystery once more held field and river.

Then a change began slowly to declare itself. The horizon became clearer, field and tree came more into sight, and somehow with a different look; the mystery began to drop away from them. A bird piped suddenly, and was still; and a light breeze sprang up and set the reeds and bulrushes rustling. Rat, who was in the stern of the boat, while Mole sculled, sat up suddenly and listened with a passionate intentness. Mole, who with gentle strokes was just keeping the boat moving while he scanned the banks with care, looked at him with curiosity.

'It's gone!' sighed the Rat, sinking back in his seat again. 'So beautiful and strange and new! Since it was to end so soon, I almost wish I had never heard it. For it has roused a longing in me that is pain, and nothing seems worth while but just to hear that sound once more and go on listening to it for ever. No! There it is again!' he cried, alert once more. Entranced, he was silent for a long space, spellbound.

'Now it passes on and I begin to lose it,' he said presently. 'O, Mole! the

Mapledurham Mill: 'Leaving the main stream they passed into what seemed at first like a little landlocked lake . . . ahead of them the silvery shoulder and foamy tumble of a weir, arm-in-arm with a restless, dripping mill-wheel that held up in its turn a grey-gabled mill-house, filled the air with a soothing murmur of sound, dull and smothery, yet with little clear voices speaking up cheerfully at intervals. Mole could only hold up both fore-paws and gasp, "Oh my! Oh my!"' The Wind in the Willows

beauty of it! The merry bubble and joy, the thin, clear, happy call of the distant piping! Such music I never dreamed of, and the call in it is stronger even than the music is sweet! Row on, Mole, row! For the music and the call must be for us.'

The Mole, greatly wondering, obeyed. 'I hear nothing myself,' he said, 'but the wind playing in the reeds and rushes and osiers.'

The Rat never answered, if indeed he heard. Rapt, transported, trembling, he was possessed in all his senses by this new divine thing that caught up his helpless soul and swung and dandled it, a powerless but happy infant in a strong sustaining grasp.

In silence the Mole rowed steadily, and soon they came to a point where the river divided, a long backwater branching off to one side. With a slight movement of his head Rat, who had long dropped the rudder-lines, directed the rower to take the backwater. The creeping tide of light gained and gained, and now they could see the colour of the flowers that gemmed the water's edge.

'Clearer and nearer still,' cried the Rat joyously. 'Now you must surely hear it! Ah – at last – I see you do!'

Breathless and transfixed the Mole stopped rowing as the liquid run of that glad piping broke on him like a wave, caught him up, and possessed him utterly. He saw the tears on his comrade's cheeks, and bowed his head and understood. For a space they hung there, brushed by the purple loosestrife that fringed the bank; then the clear imperious summons that marched hand-in-hand with the intoxicating melody imposed its will on Mole, and mechanically he bent to his oars again. And the light grew steadily stronger, but no birds sang as they were wont to do at the approach of dawn; and but for the heavenly music all was marvellously still.

On either side of them, as they glided onwards, the rich meadow-grass seemed that morning of a freshness and a greenness unsurpassable. Never had they noticed the roses so vivid, the willow-herb so odorous and pervading. Then the murmur of the approaching weir began to hold the air, and they felt a consciousness that they were nearing the end, whatever it might be, that surely awaited their expedition.

A wide half-circle of foam and glinting lights and shining shoulders of green water, the great weir closed the backwater from bank to bank, troubled all the quiet surface with twirling eddies and floating foam-streaks, and deadened all other sounds with its solemn and soothing rumble. In midmost of the stream, embraced in the weir's shimmering arm-spread, a small island lay anchored, fringed with willow and silver birch and alder. Reserved, shy, but full of significance, it hid whatever it might hold behind a veil, keeping it till the hour should come, and, with the hour, those who were called and chosen.

Slowly, but with no doubt or hesitation whatever, and in something of a solemn expectancy, the two animals passed through the broken, tumultuous water and moored their boat at the flowery margin of the island. In silence they landed, and pushed through the blossom and scented herbage and undergrowth that led up to the level ground, till they stood on a little lawn of marvellous green, set round with Nature's own orchard-trees – crab-apple, wild cherry, and sloe.

'This is the place of my song-dream, the place the music played to me,' whispered the Rat, as if in a trance. 'Here, in this holy place, here if anywhere, surely we shall find Him!'

Then suddenly the Mole felt a great Awe fall upon him, an awe that turned his muscles to water, bowed his head, and rooted his feet to the ground. It was no panic terror – indeed he felt wonderfully at peace and happy – but it was an awe that smote and held him and, without seeing, he knew it could only mean that some august Presence was very, very near. With difficulty he turned to look for his friend, and saw him at his side cowed, stricken, and trembling violently. And still there was utter silence in the populous bird-haunted branches around them; and still the light grew and grew.

. . . Trembling he raised his humble head; and then, in that utter clearness of the imminent dawn, while Nature, flushed with fullness of incredible colour, seemed to hold her breath for the event, he looked in the very eyes of the Friend and Helper; saw the backward sweep of the curved horns gleaming in the growing daylight; saw the stern, hooked nose between the kindly eyes that were looking down on him humorously, while the bearded mouth broke into a half-smile at the corners; saw the rippling muscles on the arm that lay across the broad chest, the long supple hand still holding the pan-pipes only just fallen away from the parted lips; saw the splendid curves of the shaggy limbs disposed in majestic ease on the sward; saw, last of all, nestling between his very hooves, sleeping soundly in entire peace and contentment, the little, round, podgy, childish form of the baby otter. All this he saw, for one moment breathless and intense, vivid on the

morning sky; and still, as he looked, he lived; and still, as he lived, he wondered.

'Rat!' he found breath to whisper, shaking. 'Are you afraid?'

'Afraid?' murmured the Rat, his eyes shining with unutterable love. 'Afraid of HIM?' O, never, never! And yet – and yet – O, Mole, I am afraid!'

Then the two animals, crouching to the earth, bowed their heads and did worship.

A L Rowse

b. 1903

'It seemed that time stood still, that for a moment time was held up and one saw experience as through a rift across the flow of it, a shaft into the universe.'

Poet, biographer and historian, Alfred Leslie Rowse, was born in 1903 in Tregonissey, East Cornwall, a village now wholly part of St Austell.

Rowse recalls in his memoir, 'A Cornish Childhood', that Tregonissey was a village 'half-way up the hillside to the north-east from the town of St Austell to the china-clay uplands', great mountains of clay, a landscape with a strange fascination of its own.

His father was a clay worker on less than £1 a week. In those days mining families enjoyed the same kind of solidarity, the same unity, the same kind of integrity with the land that subsisted among the tin miners of Cornwall for centuries before. They were its culture.

In the pre-war years of which I am writing . . . the family names which for generations and even for centuries had belonged to some particular spot had not as yet been disturbed, uprooted by the revolution in transport. Though many Cornish families sent a large quota of their sons abroad . . . the parent stock remained at home in the old place. So there were always Jenkinses at Phernyssick, Pascoes at Holmbush, Tretheweys at Roche; Kellows, Blameys, Rowses at Tregonissey. Now as I write, there is neither a Kellow nor a Blamey nor a Rowse at Tregonissey any more. The old structure has at length been broken, like a pitcher at the well, the pieces dispersed . . .

The village was a straggle of houses along one side of the road, where for a bit it was level before mounting the hill to Lane End, then to Carclaze, then Penwithick, with which you were in the Higher Quarter proper. The other side of the road – it was no more than a ribbon of a lane, with high hedges on either side and many twists and bends, very convenient for the game of frightening people, which was much to the fore as an amusement in that simple society – was bordered by elms; so that the village had a not unattractive appearance in my early years, with its cob-walled cottages washed yellow and cream, the colour of the clotted cream on top of the pans in the dairy at the farm. A few were a deeper shade, saffron. A little group of thatched cottages in the middle of the village had a small orchard attached; and I remember well the peculiar purity of the blue sky seen through the white clusters of apple-blossom in spring. I remember being moon-struck looking at it one morning early on my way to school. It meant something for me; what I couldn't say. It gave me an unease at heart, some reaching out towards perfection such as impels men into religion, some sense of the

The Tregonissey of Arthur Rowse's childhood. He is standing in front of the gabled porch next to his elder brother George. The Rowses had the grocer's shop (two-thirds of the way along, showing a lot of roof), where Arthur would help with the accounts.

transcendence of things, of the fragility of our hold upon life, mixed up with a schoolboy's dream of an earlier world (I was then reading Q's 'The Splendid Spur') of England in the time of the Civil War, the gallant bands of young horsemen careering out in the morning, Spring, the pure sunlight falling over the hills in waves under that cloudless blue. It was always morning, early morning, in that day-dream – and here I was, a schoolboy loitering a little, hugging that experience, incapable then of describing it to anyone, even myself, on my way to school.

I could not know then that it was an early taste of aesthetic sensation, a kind of revelation which has since become a secret touchstone of experience for me, an inner resource and consolation. Later on, though still a schoolboy – now removed downhill to the secondary school – when I read Wordsworth's 'Tintern Abbey' and 'Intimations of Immortality', I realised that that was the experience he was writing about. In time it became my creed – if that word can be used of a religion which has no dogma; for with this ultimate aesthetic experience, this apprehension of the world and life as having value essentially in the moment of being apprehended *qua* beauty, I had no need of religion . . . nothing of all that corresponded with my inner experience.

Years later at Oxford, when I had just ceased to be an undergraduate and had some time as a young Fellow of All Souls to look round and reflect in, I

'I remember well the peculiar purity of the blue sky seen through the white clusters of apple-blossom in spring. I remember being moon-struck looking at it one morning early on my way to school.'

tried to think it out for myself. I was trying to determine what gave value to an experience and in what the value of this consisted, since to me it represented the ultimate secretion of value in my universe. It semed to me, after no very long but most intense reflection – I remembered no more intense effort of thought – that what was characteristic of the experience was that in the moment of undergoing it, in contemplating the light come and go upon the facade of a building, the moon setting behind St Mary's spire outside my window – Newman's St Mary's – in listening to Beethoven or Byrd, or seeing the blue sky through the apple-blossom of my childhood, in that very moment it seemed that time stood still, that for a moment time was held up and one saw experience as through a rift across the flow of it, a shaft into the universe. But what gave such poignancy to the experience was that, in the very same moment as one felt time standing still, one knew at the back of the mind, or with another part of it, that it was moving inexorably on, carrying oneself and life with it. So that the acuity of the experience, the reason why it moved one so profoundly, was that at bottom it was a protest of the personality against the realisation of its final extinction.

One other memory dates back to this very early time . . . one of those moments with all

The glory and the freshness of a dream

which redeem life, and give me a standard, a touchstone by which to estimate all the rest . . . It was a still evening in early summer, for the bluebells were out in Doctor's fields up on the hill-side. And it was a Sunday evening, for we were all walking in the fields together, a very rare event: I never remember it happening again. As we walked, we picked bluebells in the cool of the evening. And then from far over the shoulder of the hill-side to the west there came the silvery sound of the bells of St Mewan ringing to church, so rare a sound, so far away, we very rarely heard them, like church-bells in a dream on a May morning. The thought of those bells brings tears to my eyes; their memory speaks to me of my buried childhood, brings back that moment in the cool of the evning, the bluebells gathered, the thorn hedges in leaf, father and mother and the children that we were for once at one, my father now dead, all of us scattered, the unity broken.

'It was a still evening in early summer, for the bluebells were out in Doctor's fields up on the hill-side.'

Alison Uttley

b. 1884

'The quietness of the night became intense . . . She knew now that the earth was alive, the rocks were living beings, immortals were around her.'

Alison Uttley, author of many popular books but perhaps best known for her creations, Little Grey Rabbit and Sam Pig, was born Alison Jane Taylor, on December 17th, 1884, in a snow storm at Castle Top Farm, which her family occupied for some two hundred years and still stands near Cromford in Derbyshire. 'Snow was part of my life,' she would write, 'and it would always attract me, magic of fairy-tale, and snow crystals and miracles of ice flowers on the windows.'

Castle Top Farm under snow, as the day when Alison Uttley was born: 'Snow was part of my life and it would always attract me, magic of fairy-tale, and snow crystals and miracles of ice flowers on the windows.'

Fortunately for the residents of Castle Top today, the farm is not easy to find, and there is plenty to keep at bay the myriad tourists to this part of Derbyshire – a peculiarly satisfying blend of beauty and some-time industrial might. In the valley below, amongst other distractions, Gulliver's Kingdom awaits. . .

That today's residents – occupants for the past thirty-five years – have preserved Castle Top virtually as it was in Alison's day is not, as is the case at Beatrix Potter's old house at Near Sawrey in Cumbria and countless other properties on the literary trail, with the idea of museumising it, but, quite clearly, because they share in her appreciation of its sheer beauty.

'He threw away the Taylors' old midden seat when we had nowhere to store the elderberry wine,' Mrs C tells me about her husband, but there are no recriminations, the only real regret being for the giant house-leek that has grown for well over a century on the sloping roof of the pig-cotes but is, year by year, for some inexplicable reason, slipping towards the ground. Regret stems not from sentiment, just a dislike of seeing things needlessly passing away – they have a horse that is thirty-two years old and a blind dog called Butch, much loved, who must have known the horse almost half that time. Even the sheep shading themselves beneath one of Alison's favourite trees seem to be personal friends. If this is what life on a farm was like for Alison Uttley, I begin to see why she hated the pig-killing so.

It is a happy place, made periodically even happier by Mrs C's grandchildren who enjoy everything just as Susan Garland, as Alison named herself in her fictionalised autobiography, once did. The pseudonym enabled Alison to write her story in the third person, and there is a sense in which that is the only way to write about one's own childhood, so different a person does the child seem.

For Susan, Castle Top (re-named Windystone Hall) was a magical place. Having no friends of her own – (the farm is that remote, there were no other children to play with) – instinctively she imbued every living thing with a spirit of its own.

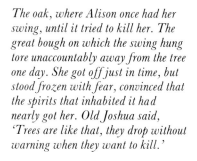

The oak, where Alison once had her swing, until it tried to kill her. The great bough on which the swing hung tore unaccountably away from the tree one day. She got off just in time, but stood frozen with fear, convinced that the spirits that inhabited it had nearly got her. Old Joshua said, 'Trees are like that, they drop without warning when they want to kill.'

A place untouched by time, 'built of the rock on which it stood . . . The farm looked like an island of fruitfulness, a small Paradise, on a shelf all to itself, with the ground falling or rising on every side.'

Trees had always had a strange fascination for Susan, ever since she had lain, an infant wrapped up in a shawl, in a clothes-basket in the orchard, babbling to the apple trees and listening to their talk. They are queer, half-human creatures, alive yet tied to the ground. Lucky they are tied, too, for rooted they are safe.

One night Susan dreamed she saw a company of mighty trees, beeches, oaks, and elms of prodigious size, walk over the sky-line, sweeping down the hills to the fields, a giant assemblage of shining ones with branches waving like a hundred arms, vast trunks moving serenely but terribly, and green hair of leaves shaking in the wind . . .

She awoke in great fear, and told her dream the next day. Margaret [her mother] called it nonsense, a nightmare, but Tom [her father] looked serious, he knew the trees, and had heard a cry when the woodmen cut down the great oak where the plantation now stood, a cry of anguish . . .

Every day she had this ordeal, a walk of a mile or more through the dense old wood, along the deserted footpath. A hundred years ago, before the highway was made, it was a well-worn road between the villages of Raddle and distant Mellow. Now it only went to Windystone Hall, and everyone walked or drove along the turnpike by the river, deep in the valley, two hundred feet below.

She walked along the rough path, casting fearful glances to right and left. She never ran, even in moments of greatest terror, when things seemed very near, for then They would know she was afraid and close around her.

No one ever knew Susan's fears, she never even formulated them to herself, except as 'things'. But whether they were giants which she half expected to see straddle out of the dark distance, or dwarfs hidden behind the trees, or bears and Indians in the undergrowth, or even the trees marching down upon her, she was not certain. They must never be mentioned, and, above all, They must never know she was afraid.

It was no use for her to tell herself there were no giants, or that bears had disappeared in England centuries ago, or that trees could not walk. She knew that quite well, but the terror remained, a subconscious fear which quickly rose to consciousness when she pressed back the catch of the gate at

The girls at school would ask her, 'Aren't you afraid to walk through the wood alone, at night?'
She never let them know her fears, though 'once, two years ago, when she was seven, a pair of eyes had looked at her.'

the entrance to the wood, and closed it soundlessly, as she entered the deep listening wood on her way home from school in the dusky evenings.

In the middle of Dark Wood the climbing path rose up a steep incline, too steep for Susan to hurry, with black shadows on either side. Then it skirted a

field, a small, queer, haunted-looking field of ragwort and bracken, long given to the wild wood, which pressed in on every side. A high, rudely-made wall surrounded it, through the chinks of which she was sure that eyes were watching. To pass this field was the culmination of agony, for she had to walk close to the wall in the semi-darkness of overhanging trees, and nothing could save her if a long arm and skinny hand shot out.

One way led downhill to a cottage in the fields below the wood, a path no one used. The other went up the steep sides of the wood past great boulders which lay among the trees like primitive beasts crouching in the dark, until it faded away to nothing in the bracken.

But something was behind the oak tree, hidden, lurking, and the leaves all watched her approach. She threw back her head and stared boldly at it, but her feet were winged for flight as she slipped softly along. Once, two years ago, when she was seven, a pair of eyes had looked at her from behind the tree, and once a dead white cow had lain there, swollen and stiff, brought to be buried in the wood.

She held her head sideways, pretending to look up at the scrap of sky, but her eyes were peeping behind, like a scared rabbit's, and the tree seemed to turn its branches and look after her, whilst the thing, whatever it was, skipped round the trunk to the other side. She never turned to look behind

Going to school through the wood in the morning sunlight was altogether different. Then, 'she felt free and careless as a squirrel or one of the brown birds flitting across the fields, very different from the wary watchful child who tried to slip through the wood unseen at night.'

The view up the kitchen garden towards the little white gate, which Alison would have had from her 'damp moss-covered seat' among the herbs.

her, but trusted to her sense of hearing, which had become very acute with the strain imposed upon it. She whispered a little prayer, a cry to God for help, as she left the tree behind.

The kitchen garden was a pleasant hiding-place, and one in which she had never been found.

Susan sat hiding on the damp moss-covered seat at the end of the garden between the sage and the herb garden. No one could see her there, for the bush of sage was like a small tree.

She had come to sit and think, about trees and God, and hell, about animals talking and what was over the edge of the world. She knew she should be in the house helping, and she was deliberately sinning.

Waves of wormwood, rue, and fennel spread round her, sharpening her senses, clearing her head with their bitter smells.

She thought of the trees she loved, the ancient yews, guarding the house, which she had never ventured to climb, for they were sacred and poison, and not to be trifled with. There were the ash trees, knee-deep in buttercups, delicate, unearthly, soft-moving, and the friendly beech trees with swings in their low boughs.

She thought of the fierce unfriendly trees in the wood, whispering and

muttering . . .

Then she wondered about animals talking. She could make everything understand, but not always could she get her answer. Animals' talk was silent, it came from their eyes, but the talk of things, of rooms and trees and fields came when she was very, very quiet and listened until they seemed to come alive . . .

Then she thought of enemies – the fox, one of the cows, an armchair, and Old Mother Besom, the witch.

'Susan! Susan! Susan!'

Margaret's voice thrilled all the garden and broke the silence into little

One day Alison decided to find a way back home from school without going through the wood: 'I started off on this adventure, skirting the bottom of the hill . . . climbing . . . clambering . . . Then I came to a miracle of loveliness. There was a stretch of

grass on that hillside blue as the sky with wild hyacinths . . . The world seemed made of flowers. The earth was azure as the sky above. I was in an Aladdin cave of treasures, open to the sky . . . I was in an Eden.'

pieces like splintering glass. Susan made an involuntary movement of obedience and repressed it.

'Susan! Susan! Come and peel the potatoes.'

Steps were approaching across the grass, the garden gate banged and Mrs Garland hurried down the path. She stooped to ·pick some thyme and a bunch of parsley bordering the stones. Then she sighed deeply and went out again.

Susan sat very still. She looked up at the sky. The morning air was sweet with the smell of the great woods which were only a few yards away, over the wall and across a dell. Little clouds looked like the petals of one of the roses on the house.

And did God live up there? But He was here too, in the garden, and she was sinning. God had seen her, His eye saw everything. Then He would know she didn't want to peel the potatoes, not today. She would go to hell if she died now, but if she lived till she had said her prayers tonight she would be safe once more. Suppose God struck her dead for her sin, and she dropped down among the rue and fennel. She looked down at her buttoned boots and wondered if she would have time to tuck them under her. Boots didn't look nice, sticking out like the cow's legs. But no one would ever find her here, no one came to the end of the garden unless they were having roast pork. It would be a long time to wait, she had better say a prayer now.

Pantheism with a Gothic edge seems perfectly at home in the mind of a lonely imaginative child among all that beauty at Castle Top. In fact Susan's God is the Christian God, whom she learns about at school and church. Not so the novelist, Forrest Reid, whose mystical childhood intuitions seem scientific by comparison, a vision of life in process seen through a powerful microscope –

The thick mossy grass was softer than a carpet under my feet. There was a little wind, but not much, and it was warm and scented. There were daffodils, and where the trees were not already clothed with green their branches were covered with buds. The rhododendrons were covered with buds, too, moist and sticky and bursting with life. Life was everywhere – in the insects, in the birds – colour, joy, ecstasy, music, the mystery of procreation, the mystery of growth and growing things, a kind of intoxication that came with the wind, the scent of the flowers and shrubs and grasses, the heat of the sun; and I felt it all thrilling in my blood as I lifted my head and shook the raindrops down from a dark cedar branch over my face and throat, while my skin tingled deliciously at the wet, cool little touches. It was the rapturous fermentation of Spring that I felt, swelling and bursting, piercing up through the brown earth, breaking into flower – breaking into a flame of intense blue that burned and blazed and splashed all over the lush green of the deeper hollows. I drew the air down into my lungs and raised my voice in my own kind of hymn.

from 'Apostate' by Forrest Reid

Others, interesting because they engender not only sunny,

'Life was everywhere . . . colour, joy, ecstasy, music, the mystery of growth and growing things, a kind of intoxication that came with the wind, the scent of the flowers and shrubs and grasses, the heat of the sun. . .'
Forrest Reid

intoxicating, escapist images, bursting with the sap of life, but also Wordsworthian 'gloom and tumult', seem to plumb deeper mysteries. 'Joy' takes in the possibility of both life and death, and the experience is one of Old Testament awe, even dread.

In 'Surprised By Joy', C S Lewis, most widely known as author of 'The Lion, The Witch and The Wardrobe', describes three landmark experiences in his childhood which were, in later life, to motivate a spiritual journey from atheism to Christianity. The crucial one is as follows:

I had become fond of Longfellow's 'Saga of King Olaf'; fond of it in a casual, shallow way for its story and its vigorous rhythms. But then, and quite different from such pleasures, and like a voice from far more distant regions, there came a moment when I idly turned the pages of the book and found the unrhymed translation of 'Tegner's Drapa' and read –

> *I heard a voice that cried*
> *Balder the beautiful*
> *Is dead; is dead –*

I knew nothing about Balder; but instantly I was uplifted into huge regions of northern sky, I desired with almost sickening intensity something never to be described (except that it is cold, spacious, severe, pale, and remote) and then, as in the other examples, found myself at the very same moment already falling out of that desire and wishing I were back in it.

The joy he experiences is described as an unsatisfied desire more desirable than any satisfaction can be, a longing, a kind of unhappiness or grief, but a kind that we want, never in our power but visited upon us. Joy is distinct from any other pleasure; it must have 'the stab, the pang', the inconsolable longing. It is a heroic concept; an intuition of mythic status.

No longer a child, but while still a youth, long after the memory of Balder had vanished from his mind, his early experience is suddenly recalled:

Someone must have left in the schoolroom a literary periodical . . . My eye fell upon a headline and a picture, carelessly, expecting nothing. A moment later, as the poet says, 'The sky had turned round.'

What I had read was the words 'Siegfried and the Twilight of the Gods'. What I had seen was one of Arthur Rackham's illustrations to that volume. I had never heard of Wagner, nor of Siegfried . . .

Pure 'Northernness' engulfed me: a vision of huge, clear spaces hanging above the Atlantic in the endless twilight of Northern summer, remoteness, severity . . . and almost at the same moment I knew that I had met this before, long, long ago (it hardly seems longer now) in 'Tegner's Drapa', that Siegfried (whatever it might be) belonged to the same world as Balder and the sunward-sailing cranes. And with that plunge back into my own past there arose at once, almost like heartbreak, the memory of Joy itself . . .

The extraordinary thing about this stage in C S Lewis's conversion to Christianity is the sheer harshness of the image which leads him – it is 'dreadful', in its archaic sense. Lewis's joy is not the warm image of a merciful loving Christian God (in fact his passage to Christianity from atheism passes through an intermediate theistic stage), but an image born out of ancient myth, calling to mind the icy grounds of the legendary Castle of Arianrhod where –

> *Incomprehensible numbers there were*
> *Maintained in a chilly hell*
> *Until the Fifth Age of the world,*
> *Until Christ should release the captives.*

The Castle of Arianrhod was a chilly purgatory situated in the Corona Borealis, the mythic Kingdom of Lost Souls, Land of the Dead, ruled over, it was believed, by the Goddess Ariadne, younger self of the Moon Goddess.

In ancient myth the Moon Goddess was the ultimate goddess, the first and last. Before the Greeks and Romans proliferated their male demi-gods, she represented the ultimate creative and procreative force. The ancient Pelasgian Creation myth centred upon her as Eurynome. The Pelasgians were a people for whom the idea of a male god of creation would have seemed absurd. Procreation was a feminine principle.

Combining all things and their opposites within her in the name of truth, the Goddess represented both beauty and terror, both kindness and cruelty, both life and death. She was both sides of nature's coin, because in truth there is no one-sided coin.

'Pure "Northernness" engulfed me: a vision of huge, clear spaces hanging over the Atlantic in the endless twilight of Northern summer, remoteness, severity . . . and there arose at once, almost like heartbreak, the memory of Joy itself.' C S Lewis

The Moon Goddess was the personification of all nature: Evil and Good, Darkness and Light, and this tyrannous economy is what seduces the aesthetic judgement of the true Muse poet. As poetic Muse she was celebrated by Robert Graves in his historic grammar of poetic myth, The White Goddess.

The Goddess's chillier, awesome aspect two poets later show us as their 'tragic need'. For now it is intriguing to note how often imaginative childhood visions incorporate either the Moon herself or her awesome majesty. The following is part of a seminal childhood vision received by the writer Gavin Maxwell from his memoir, 'The House of Elrig':

In the foreground a polar bear stood heraldic on an ice-flow; the sea around it was deep blue, fathomless with secrets, and across the vast background of ink-blue sky flamed a stupendous curtain of multi-coloured aurora borealis. I was drawn into a majesty of icy desolation and loneliness, of limitless space and aweful splendour, colder and remoter than the stars, so that my throat tightened and I wanted to cry because it was so beautiful and terrible.

Herbert Read writes of the child's 'natural craving for horrors', but C S Lewis and Gavin Maxwell take us into another stratum of experience altogether. Oddly, it is to the moon that even little Susan Garland eventually gives herself wholeheartedly up.

It is the witching hour, the white light of the moon pulls her ('as it pulled the earth'), out of bed, down creaking stairs, through a ghost-filled kitchen, and out onto the lawn, where she stands, with cold wet feet, looking up. Suddenly her Christian God is nowhere to be seen; the scene is still quite sweet, but it *is* complete surrender.

No God was there, only the bright face of the moon, very near the earth; she felt she could touch him if she had a ladder.

Something rustled in the ivy bushes, perhaps a bird, moving in his sleep, tucking his head afresh under his wing. But she kept her eyes on the moon as if she were caught in a web hanging through the air, dipping down and up again, thinking of nothing, unconscious of time, surrendering herself to the flood of light. A great peace floated round her and happiness wrapped her.

She felt the earth swimming through space, as she had felt it before, swinging past the stars, on through the dark sky, and the moon came too . . .

The quietness of the night became intense, she could hear her heart beating and she thought it was the earth's. She knew now that the earth was alive, the rocks were living beings, immortals were around her. So that was what the moon wanted to tell her.

The old house behind her seemed to stir and try to speak to her. She turned to it and stretched out a hand.

The moon slipped into a cloud like a fish into a net, and a shadow fell over the earth.

W H Hudson

b. 1841

'The sense of mystery would grow until a sensation of delight would change to fear, and the fear increase until it was no longer to be borne.'

William Henry Hudson, the novelist and writer on nature – his book, 'A Shepherd's Life', about Caleb Bawcombe, who spent all seasons, night and day, with his sheep and dogs and the people of the Wiltshire downs, is an enduring classic – was born on a farm in the pampass plain near Buenos Aires.

As a small boy of six but well able to ride bare-backed at a fast gallop without falling off, I invite the reader, mounted too, albeit on nothing but an imaginary animal, to follow me a league or so from the gate to some spot where the land rises to a couple or three or four feet above the surrounding level. There, sitting on our horses, we shall command a wider horizon than even the tallest man would have standing on his own legs, and in this way get a better idea of the district in which ten of the most impressionable years of my life, from five to fifteen, were spent.

We see all round us a flat land, its horizon as perfect ring of misty blue colour where the crystal-dome of the sky rests on the level green world . . . there were smooth areas where sheep had pastured, but the surface varied greatly and was mostly more or less rough. In places the land as far as one could see was covered with a dense growth of cardoon thistles, or wild artichoke, of a bluish or grey-green colour, while in other places the giant thistle flourished, a plant with big variegated green and white leaves, and standing when in flower six to ten feet high. On all this visible earth there were no fences, and no trees excepting those which had been planted at the old estancia houses.

Very, very early in my boyhood I had acquired the habit of going about alone to amuse myself in my own way, and it was only after years, when my age was about twelve, that my mother told me how anxious this singularity in me used to make her. She would miss me when looking out to see what the children were doing, and I would be called and searched for, to be found hidden away somewhere in the plantation. Then she began to keep an eye on me, and when I was observed stealing off she would secretly follow and watch me, standing motionless among the tall weeds or under the trees by the half-hour . . . This distressed her very much; then to her great relief and joy she discovered that I was there with a motive she could understand and appreciate: that I was watching some living thing, an insect perhaps, but oftener a bird – a pair of little scarlet flycatchers building a nest of lichen on a peach tree, or some such beautiful thing.

One hot day in December I had been standing perfectly still for a few minutes among the dry weeds when a slight rustling sound came from near

'A flat land, its horizon a perfect ring of misty blue colour where the crystal dome of the sky rests on the level green world. In places the land as far as one could see was covered with a dense growth of cardoon thistles or wild artichokes.'

my feet, and glancing down I saw the head and neck of a large black serpent moving slowly past me – so slowly that it hardly appeared to move, and as the creature must have been not less than six feet long, and probably more, it took a very long time, while I stood thrilled with terror, not daring to make the slightest movement, gazing down upon it. As it moved on over the white ground it had the appearance of a coal-black current flowing past me – a current not of water or other liquid but of some such element as quicksilver moving on in a rope-like stream. At last it vanished and turning I fled from the ground.

The image of that black mysterious serpent was always in my mind from the moment of waking in the morning until I fell asleep at night. I simply could not keep away from it; the desire to look again at that strange being was too strong. I began to visit the place again, day after day, and would hang about the borders of the weedy ground watching and listening, and still no black serpent appeared. Then one day I ventured, though in fear and trembling, to go right in among the weeds, and still finding nothing began to advance step by step until I was right in the middle of the weedy ground. All I wanted was just to see it once more, and I had made up my mind that immediately on its appearance, if it did appear, I would take to my heels. It was then when standing in this central spot that once again that slight rustling sound reached my straining sense and sent an icy chill down my back. And there, within six inches of my toes, appeared the black head and neck, followed by the long, seemingly endless body. I dared not move, since to have attempted flight might have been fatal. The weeds were thinnest here, and the black head and slow-moving black coil could be followed by the eye for a little distance. About a yard from me there was a hole in the ground about the circumference of a breakfast cup at the top, and into this hole the serpent put his head and slowly, slowly drew himself in, while I stood waiting until the whole body to the tip of the tail had vanished.

I had seen my wonderful creature, my black serpent unlike any serpent in the land, and the excitement following the first thrill of terror was still on me, but I was conscious of an element of delight in it, and I would not now resolve not to visit the spot again.

These serpent memories serve to remind me of a subject not yet mentioned in my narrative: this is *animism*, or that sense of something in nature which to the enlightened or civilised man is not there, and in the civilised man's child, if it be admitted that he has it at all, is but a faint survival of a phase of the primitive mind. And by animism I do not mean the theory of a soul in nature, but the tendency or impulse or instinct, in which all myth originates, to animate things; the projection of ourselves into nature; the sense and apprehension of an intelligence like our own but more powerful in all visible things. It persists and lives in many of us, I imagine, more than we like to think, or more than we know, especially in those born and bred amidst rural surroundings, where there are hills and woods and rocks and streams and waterfalls, these being conditions which are most favourable to it.

In large towns and all populous places, where nature has been tamed until it appears like a part of man's work, almost as artificial as the buildings he inhabits, it withers and dies so early in life that its faint intimations are soon forgotten and we come to believe that we have never experienced them. That such a feeling can survive in any man, or that there was ever a time since his infancy when he could have regarded this visible world as anything but what it 'actually is' – the stage to which he has been summoned to play his brief but important part, with painted blue and green scenery for background – becomes incredible. Nevertheless, I know that in me, old as I am, this same primitive faculty which manifested itself in my early boyhood, still persists, and in those early years was so powerful that I am almost afraid to say how deeply I was moved by it.

It is difficult, impossible I am told, for anyone to recall his boyhood exactly as it was. It could not have been what it seems to the adult mind, since we cannot escape from what we are, however great our detachment may be; and in going back we must take our present selves with us.

I only know that my memory takes me back to a time when the delight I experienced in all natural things was purely physical. I rejoiced in colours, scents, sounds, in taste and touch: the blue of the sky, the verdure of the earth, the sparkle of sunlight on water, the taste of milk, of fruit, of honey, the smell of dry or moist soil, of wind and rain, of herbs and flowers; the mere feel of a blade of grass made me happy; and there were certain sounds and perfumes, and above all certain colours in flowers, and in the plumage and eggs of birds, such as the purple polished shell of the tinamou's egg, which intoxicated me with delight.

'The sight of a magnificent sunset was sometimes more than I could endure and made me wish to hide myself away.'

It was not, I think, till my eighth year that I began to be distinctly conscious of something more than this mere childish delight in nature. It may have been there all the time in infancy – I don't know; but when I began to know it consciously it was as if some hand had surreptitiously dropped something into the honeyed cup which gave it at certain times a new flavour. It gave me little thrills, often purely pleasurable, at other times startling, and there were occasions when it became so poignant as to frighten me. The sight of a magnificent sunset was sometimes almost more than I could endure and made me wish to hide myself away. But when the feeling was roused by the sight of a small and beautiful or singular object, such as a flower, its sole effect was to intensify the object's loveliness.

There were many flowers which produced this effect in but a slight degree, and as I grew up and the animistic sense lost its intensity, these too lost their magic and were almost like other flowers which had never had it.

There were others which never lost what for want of a better word I have just called their magic, and of these I will give an account of one.

I was about nine years old when during one of my rambles on horseback I found at a distance of two or three miles from home, a flower that was new to me. The plant, a little over a foot in height, was growing in the shelter of some large cardoon thistle, or wild artichoke bushes. It had three stalks clothed with long narrow, sharply pointed leaves, which were downy, soft to the feel like the leaves of our great mullein, and pale green in colour. All three stems were crowned with clusters of flowers, the single flower a little larger than that of the red valerian, of a pale red hue and a peculiar shape, as each small pointed petal had a fold or twist at the end. Altogether it was slightly singular in appearance and pretty, though not to be compared with scores of other flowers of the plains for beauty. Nevertheless it had an extraordinary fascination for me, and from the moment of discovery it became one of my sacred flowers.

On first discovering it I took a spray to show to my mother, and was strangely disappointed that she, who alone seemed always to know what was in my mind and who loved all beautiful things, especially flowers, should have failed to see what I had found in it!

The feeling, however, was evoked more powerfully by trees than by even the most supernatural of my flowers; it varied in power according to time and place and the appearance of the tree or trees, and always affected me most on moonlit nights. I used to steal out of the house alone when the moon was at its full to stand, silent and motionless, near some group of large trees, gazing at the dusky green foliage silvered by the beams; and at such times the sense of mystery would grow until a sensation of delight would change to fear, and the fear increase until it was no longer to be borne, and I would hastily escape to recover a sense of reality and safety indoors, where there was light and company. Yet on the very next night I would steal out again and go to the spot where the effect was strongest.

I never spoke of these feelings to others, not even to my mother, notwithstanding that she was always in perfect sympathy with me with regard to my love of nature. The reason for my silence was, I think, my powerlessness to convey in words what I felt; but I imagine it would be correct to describe the sensation experienced on those moonlit nights among the trees as similar to the feeling a person would have if visited by a supernatural being. . .

This faculty or instinct of the dawning mind is or has always seemed to me essentially religious in character, but it was more to me in those early days than all the religious teaching I received from my mother. These teachings did not touch my heart as it was touched and thrilled by some nearer, more intimate, in nature, not only in moonlit trees or in a flower or serpent, but, in certain exquisite moments and moods.

Chapter Four: *Midsummer Joys*

**The Spring of our life – our youth – is the
midsummer of our happiness; our pleasures are
then real and heart stirring.**
John Clare

Richard Jefferies

b. 1848

'*The sun looked down on these sons of care, and all the morning beamed.*'

There was a hill to which I used to resort . . . The labour of walking three
miles to it, all the while gradually ascending, seemed to clear the blood of the
heaviness accumulated at home. On a warm summer day the slow
continued rise required continual effort, which carried away the sense of
oppression.

. . . Moving up the sweet short turf, at every step my heart seemed to
obtain a wider horizon of feeling; with every inhalation of rich pure air, a
deeper desire. The very light of the sun was whiter and more brilliant here.
By the time I had reached the summit I had entirely forgotten the petty
circumstances and the annoyances of existence. I felt myself, myself . . .

I was utterly alone with the sun and the earth. Lying down on the grass, I
spoke in my soul to the earth, the sun, the air, and the distant sea far beyond
sight. I thought of the earth's firmness – I felt it bear me up; through the
grassy couch there came an influence as if I could feel the great earth
speaking to me. I thought of the wandering air – its pureness, which is its
beauty; the air touched me and gave me something of itself. I spoke to the
sea: though so far, in my mind I saw it, green at the rim of the earth and blue
in deeper ocean; I desired to have its strength, its mystery, and glory. Then I
addressed the sun, desiring the soul equivalent of his light and brilliance, his
endurance and unwearied race. I turned to the blue heaven over, gazing into
its depth, inhaling its exquisite colour and sweetness . . . By all these I
prayed; I felt an emotion of the soul beyond all definition; prayer is a puny
thing to it, and the word is a rude sign to the feeling, but I know no other. . .
from 'The Story of My Heart'

The 'heaviness accumulated at home' suggests that the young
Richard Jefferies entered upon so intense a relationship with
nature in response to, or perhaps as a reaction against, a
repressive home life. It is true, there were problems. James
Jefferies, Richard's father, had been a printer in London when, in
1844, upon his marriage to Elizabeth Gyde, his father, John,

offered them Coate farm, which still stands two miles from Swindon in Wiltshire, on the edge of Coate Water.

James moved with his new wife to the farm and it was understood that eventually the farm would be theirs. But when, in 1868, they inherited the estate, they discovered that John Jefferies had attached a condition to the inheritance. Legacies totalling £1,300 would have to be paid from the estate to James's two married sisters. In order to fulfil the legal requirement James had to mortgage the property.

That might not have proved crippling had James been a man with a sense of business. The farm had potential, and James had already improved the place, but his improvements (other than those insisted upon by his father, such as the construction of the rickyard buildings) were of little commercial use. The locals looked on in wonderment when James planted a copper beech, a mulberry, and other trees and shrubs in the farmhouse garden, and laughed at his stone ha-ha. It was unusual for a farmer to spend time and money laying out a formal pleasure garden instead of getting his farm up and running. And why, they wondered, did he prefer to plant a russet apple tree rather than the traditional cider apple? – 'Why wouldn't thaay a' done for he as well as for we?'

James was unmoved. He was more of a bookman than a farmer, and, like his own father, was stubborn and proud. In fact, the stories which come down to us of the Jefferies' family suggest that stubborn eccentricity and pride – a potentially difficult combination, liable to set one at odds with life – were strong family traits, at least in the male line.

Very probably old John Jefferies had put the condition on the inheritance in order to make his son more money conscious. There'd been question marks over James's ability to come good before he came to Coate, and once he had arrived he seemed to prefer to make it beautiful rather than efficient, retaining workers for their own good over that of the farm.

Richard's mother, a woman with middle-class expectations, and once described by her niece as 'town-bred', was not suited to farm life and became increasingly irritable as it dawned on her that farm business was beyond her husband and, when debts mounted, that his pride prevented him seeking help from other members of the Jefferies clan.

Richard Jefferies was born four years after his parents came to Coate and grew up in a progressively worsening family atmosphere. So bad did it become that between the ages of 4 and 9 he was sent for long periods to live with his aunt and uncle in Sydenham. But he was close to his father, who impressed upon

Coate farmhouse where Richard was born, looking past the mulberry planted by his father, which figures in several of Richard's books. The house is set mid-way between Swindon and Liddington Hill, the hill referred to in the passage from The Story of My Heart. *The oldest part of the building, a low, thatched farmhouse, dates back to around 1700. Richard's grandather inherited it in 1825 and, with the help of a hoard of gold coins found hidden in his house in Swindon, built at Coate what became the main house adjoining the old cottage.*

him a love of literature and the countryside, which seems to have offered them both a much needed avenue of escape from 'the petty circumstances and the annoyances of existence'.

Coate Water, which lies just south of the farm, covers well over fifty acres of ground. The lake, its islands, the woods, the reeded swampland with its wildlife, became not a fantasy playground for Richard, but a haven more real to him than the lie of his family life inside.

In 'Bevis: The Story of a Boy', Richard's loosely disguised childhood autobiography, Bevis (Richard) and his young friend Mark (in reality Richard's younger brother Henry) engage in a series of wonderfully imaginative outdoor adventures, most of which are centred around Coate Water, or the Longpond as they called it then.

There are adventures in the farm, on the lake and around it, by day and by the light of the stars at night. It is a happy rousing story of adventurous childhood, the prototype adventure story for boys, published almost fifty years before 'Swallows and Amazons' and two years before Arthur Ransome was even born.

It also carries plenty of evidence of its author's acute powers of observation and knowledge of nature, culled eagerly as a child from the environs of Coate, in preference, it seems, to succeeding at school.

Near the beginning of the book, Bevis and Mark re-name the Longpond, the New Sea, with their spaniel, Pan.

'Let's go round the Longpond,' said Bevis; 'we have never been quite round it.'

'So we will,' said Mark. 'But we shall not be back to dinner.'

'As if travellers ever thought of dinner! Of course we shall take our provisions with us.'

So they went in, and loaded their pockets with huge double slices of bread-and-butter done up in paper, apples, and the leg of a roast duck from the pantry. Then came the compass, an old one in a brass case; Mark broke his nails opening the case, which was tarnished, and the card at once swung round to the north, pointing to the elms across the road from the window of the sitting-room. Bevis took the bow and three arrows, made of the young wands of hazel which grow straight, and Mark was armed with a spear, a long ash rod with sharpened end, which they thrust in the kitchen fire a few minutes to harden in the proper manner.

Pan raced before them up the footpath; the gate that led to the Longpond was locked, and too high to be climbed easily, but they knew a gap, and crept through on hands and knees.

As they stood up in the field the other side, they had an anxious consultation as to what piece of water it was they were going to discover; whether it was a lake in Central Africa, or one in America.

'I'm tired of lakes,' said Mark. 'They have found out such a lot of lakes, and the canoes are always upset, and there is such a lot of mud. Let's have a new sea altogether.'

'So we will,' said Bevis. 'That's capital – we will find a new sea where no one has ever been before. Look!' – for they had now advanced to where the gleam of the sunshine on the mere was visible through the hedge – 'Look! there it is; is it not wonderful?'

To Elizabeth Jefferies, her eldest son was the least satisfactory of her four children: Richard consistently failed to show any practical application, and the more his father James became role model, the more Elizabeth despaired of Richard. She thought him lazy, a dreamer. He became known as 'Moony Dick'.

But Richard's indolence was not congenital – later, as a writer, once he had found what he wanted to do, he was to display enormous stamina for hard work. From the start he was intuitively opposed to a Victorian work ethic that turned life into a drudgery, to be rewarded with a better life in heaven. As a man, he was out of time: beauty was here and now; life was beautiful, if only people might see it. He believed in the holiness of life on earth, the eternal now, and this belief had its roots in his childhood at Coate.

Between one adventure and the next, Bevis and Mark assimilate moments of great natural beauty, not as onlookers, but without comment, as an integral part of the process. At the end of a day sailing a make-shift raft, the boys relax with Pan on a steep bank where the farm stream pours from a hatch in a mound and forms a deep pool; the boys' legs dangle over the edge above the bubbling water:

A broad, cool shadow from the trees had fallen over the hatch, for the afternoon had gone on, and the sun was declining behind them over the western hills. A broad, cool shadow, whose edges were far away, so that they were in the midst of it. The thrushes sang in the ashes, for they knew that the quiet evening, with the dew they love, was near. A bullfinch came to the hawthorn hedge just above the hatch, looked in and out once or twice, and then stepped inside the spray near his nest. A yellow-hammer called from the top of a tree, and another answered him across the field. Afar in the mowing-grass the crake lifted his voice, for he talks more as the sun sinks.

The swirling water went round and round under the fall, with lines of white bubbles rising, and quivering masses of yellowish foam ledged on the red rootlets under the bank and against the flags. The swirling water, ceaselessly beaten by the descending stream coming on it with a long-continued blow, returned to be driven away again. A steady roar of the fall, and a rippling sound above it of bursting bubbles and crossing wavelets of the hastening stream, notched and furrowed over stones, frowning in eager haste. The rushing and the coolness, and the song of the brook and the birds, and the sense of the sun sinking, stilled even Bevis and Mark a little

'That's capital – we will find a new sea where no one has ever been before. Look!' The Longpond or New Sea, Richard Jefferies' playground as a boy.

'All the strain and desperation in much of Jefferies' writings, and his sickness and premature death, can be traced to the human surroundings of his childhood, youth, and early manhood,' wrote Henry Williamson. But it was here on the sedgy banks of Coate Water that the boy found release, concocting games probably in imitation of James Fenimore Cooper's frontiersman stories ('The Last of the Mohicans', etc), which were among his father's books, games that would later produce 'Bevis' – the prototype outdoor, boy's adventure story.

while. They sat and listened, and said nothing; the delicious brook filled their ears with music.

Next minute Bevis seized Pan by the neck and pitched him over into the bubbles. . .

Henry Williamson, who did so much to recommend Richard Jefferies to a 20th-century audience, described 'Bevis' as 'the best boys' book in England' and called Richard 'a genius, a visionary whose thought and feeling were wide as the human world, prophet of an age not yet come into being – the age of sun, of harmony. . .' Such a 'rare first-class writer . . . has the keenness of a wild animal. He is natural. He is an authentic animation of the sun.'

Next morning as they went through the meadow, where the dew still lingered in the shade, on the way to the bathing-place . . . they hung about the path picking clover-heads and sucking the petals, pulling them out and putting the lesser ends in their lips, looking at the white and pink bramble flowers, noting where the young nuts began to show, pulling down the woodbine, and doing everything but hasten on to their work of swimming. . .

'We ought to be something,' said Mark discontentedly.

'Of course we ought,' said Bevis. 'Things are very stupid unless you are something.'

'Savages!' shouted Mark, kicking the gate to with a slam that startled Pan up. 'Savages, of course!'

'Why?'

'They swim, donk; don't they? They're always in the water, and they have catamarans and ride waves and dance on the shore; and blow shells –'

'Trumpets?'

'Yes.'

'Canoes?'

'Yes.'

'No clothes?'

'No.'

'All jolly?'

'Everything.'

'Hurrah!'

Away they ran to the bathing-place to be savages.

. . . By and by, while still, and looking out over the water, Bevis's quiet eye became conscious of a slight movement opposite at the mouth of the Nile. He got up, took his bow and arrows, and went to the firs. The dead, dry needles or leaves on the ground felt rough to his naked feet, and he had to take care not to step on the hard cones. A few small bramble bushes forced him to go aside, so that it took him some little time to get near the Nile.

He stopped as the ripples on the other side of the brook became visible; then gradually lifting his head, sheltered by a large alder, he traced the ripples back to the shore, under the bank, and saw a moorcock feeding by

'By and by, Bevis's quiet eye became conscious of a slight movement at the mouth of the Nile . . . He got up, took his bow and arrows, and went to the firs.'

'Bevis grasped his bow firm in his left hand, drew the arrow quick but steadily, and as the sharp point covered the bird, loosed it. There was a splash and a fluttering. . . The arrow had struck the moorcock's wing.'

the roots of a willow. Bevis waited till the cock turned his back, then he stole another step forward to the alder.

It was about ten yards to the willow, but he could not get any nearer, for there was no more cover beyond the alder – the true savage is never content unless he is close to his game. Bevis grasped his bow firm in his left hand, drew the arrow quick but steadily – not with a jerk – and as the sharp point covered the bird, loosed it. There was a splash and a fluttering, and he knew instantly that he had hit. 'Mark! Mark!' he shouted, and ran down the bank, heedless of the jagged stones. Mark heard, and came racing through the firs.

The arrow had struck the moorcock's wing, but even then the bird would have got away, for the point had no barb, and in diving and struggling it would have come out, had not he been so near the willow. The spike went through the wing and nailed it to a thick root; the arrow quivered as it was stopped by the wood. Bevis seized him by the neck and drew the arrow out.

'Kill him! Kill him!' shouted Mark. The other savage pulled the neck, and Mark, leaping down the jagged stones, took the dead bird in his eager hands.

'Here's where the arrow went in.'

'There's three feathers in the water.'

'Feel how warm he is.'

'Look at the thick red on his bill.'

'See his claws.'

'Hurrah!'

'Let's eat him.'

'Raw?'

As time went by, and boy turned adolescent, feeling ever more the outcast, Richard began to play the part in his physical appearance. He grew his hair down to his shoulders and a beard, which served further to set him apart from his contemporaries in Swindon. Those who laughed at him, he pitied for their limited view of life. At sixteen he ran away from home, intending to go to Moscow (or possibly America), but was forced by lack of funds to turn back at Liverpool.

The saddest characteristic to develop in the growing boy was an exaggerated desire always to assert himself, to hold the whip-hand in his dealings with other boys in his kingdom, the farm and at play by Coate Water.

Perhaps it was his way of countering the derision in which he was held elsewhere, though it did little to recommend him to his fellows: 'Dick was of a masterful temperament,' a contemporary once said of him, 'and though less strong than several of us in a bodily sense, his force of will was such that we had to succumb to whatever plans he chose to dictate, never choosing to be second even in the most trivial thing.'

In 'Bevis' it is only little Mark whom he can count on surely to kowtow, though on one notable occasion, in a Council of War by the big oak, which still stands on the East side of Coate Water, he does manage to persuade two gangs of youths to enact a battle of his choosing. It turns out to be a model of the boy's own dream:

'And who are we to be?' said Val. 'Saxons and Normans, or Crusaders, or King Arthur -'

'We're all to be Romans,' said Bevis.

'And who are we to be?' said Val. 'Saxons and Normans, or Crusaders, or King Arthur –'

'We're all to be Romans,' said Bevis.

'Then it will be the Civil War,' said Phil, who had read most history.

'Of course it will,' said Bevis, 'and I am to be Julius Caesar and Ted is to be Pompey.'

'I won't be Pompey,' said Ted; 'Pompey was beat.'

'You must,' said Bevis.

'I shan't.'

'But you MUST.'

'I won't be beaten.'

'I shall beat you easily.'

'The battle was fixed for the day after, and it was to begin in the evening . . . So they parted, and the oak was left in silence with the grass all trampled under it.'

The two armies gather – Bevis (Caesar), Mark (Mark Antony), Phil (Varro), Tom, Ted (Pompey), Jim, Frank, Walter, Bill, 'Charl', Val (Crassus), Bob, Cecil (Scipio), Sam, Fred, George, Harry, Michael, Jack, Andrew, Luke, and half a dozen more assemble and pick sides – rules of war are agreed – 'Only knocking and slashing,' said Bevis. 'Stabbing won't do, and arrows won't do, nor spears.' – strategies are agreed (Caesar sends Scipio and a third of his troops to outflank Pompey and capture his camp), and battle begins:

As he came running Caesar saw that the whole of Pompey's army was before them, while he had but two-thirds of his, and regretted now that he had so hastily detached Scipio's cohort. But waving his sword, he ran at the head of his men, keeping them in column. They were about a hundred yards apart, when Pompey faced about, and so short a distance was rapidly traversed.

Caesar's sword was the first to descend with a crash upon an enemy's weapon, but Antony was hardly a second later, and before they could lift to strike again, the legion behind, with a shout, pushed them by its impetus right through Pompey's line.

When Caesar Bevis stopped running, and looked round, there was a break in the enemy's army, which was divided into two parts. Bevis instantly made at the part on his left (where Phil Varro commanded), thinking, instinctively, to crush this half with all his soldiers. But as they did not know what his object was, for he had no time even to give an order, only four or five followed him. The rest paused and faced Val Crassus; and these Ted Pompey and six or seven of his men at once attacked.

Bevis met Phil Varro, and crossed swords with him. Clatter! crash! snap! thump! bang! They slashed and they warded: Bevis's shoulder was stung by a sharp blow. He struck back, and his sword sliding down Varro's, broke the cross-piece, and rapped his fingers smartly. Before Varro could hit again, two others, fighting, stumbled across and interrupted the combat.

'Keep together! Keep together!' shouted Phil Varro. 'Ted – Pompey, Pompey! Keep together!'

Slash! swish! crash! thump! 'Hit him! Now then! He's down! Hurrah!' Crash! Crack – a sword split and flew in splinters.

'Follow Bevis!' shouted Mark. 'Stick to Bevis! Fred! Bill! Quick!' He had privately arranged with these two, Fred and Bill, who were the biggest on their side, that all three should keep close to Bevis and form a guard . . .

Whirling his sword with terribly fury, Caesar Bevis had cut his way through all between. Slight as he was, the intense energy within him carried him through the ranks. He struck a sword from one; overthrew another rushing against him, sent a third on his knees, and reaching Phil, hit him on the arm so heavy a blow that, for a moment, he could not use the weapon, but gave way and got behind his men.

'Hurray!' shouted Mark. 'Follow Bevis! Stick to Bevis!'

Richard Jefferies' need to be recognised as leader never left him, though it remained tragically unfulfilled. Henry Williamson opened his introduction to 'Bevis' with these words: 'Richard Jefferies was a poor man who in moments of inspiration believed himself to be a prophetic thinker and writer of the world. The world did not think so.'

The irony is that his nature writing, in which he put his own self aside and became absorbed wholly in the minutiae of nature – a caterpillar making its way slowly up an almost invisible thread, a speckled trout lying immobile in the shadow of a bridge – won him most acclaim.

The Council oak.

The battle of Pharsalia, as it was called, concludes with a private duel between Caesar and Pompey. Ted throws Bevis down a cliff in the quarry and rushes off, thinking he has killed him. As the evening draws in and a storm brews Caesar and Pompey are still missing. It is Bevis's finest hour – he has taken to the New Sea in an old, leaking punt:

When Bevis felt that he was really out on the New Sea a wild delight possessed him. He shouted and sang how –

> *Estmere threw his harp aside*
> *And swith he drew his brand!*

The dash of the waves, the 'wish' of the gust as it struck him, the flying foam, the fury of the storm, the red sun almost level with the horizon towards which he drifted, the dark heaving waters in their wrath lifted his spirit to meet them. All he wished was that Mark was with him to share the pleasure. He was now in the broadest part of the New Sea, where the rollers having come so far rose yet higher. Bevis shouted to them, wild as the waves.

It was all a dream. After having initial success as a writer, Richard died aged only thirty-eight, rejected by the Age with which he was so at odds, poor and in great pain.

At the end so self-oppressed and difficult had he become that his doctors dismissed the symptoms of pain and body-wasting in his final illness (tuberculosis and ulcerated intestines) as an expression of hysterical hypochondria.

Robert Louis Stevenson

b. 1850

'I have never again been happy in the same way . . . The sense of sunshine, of green leaves, and the singing of birds, seems never to have been so strong in me as in that place.'

'It is questionable if there is any central image in an artist's work which did not come to him as a moment of vision in childhood,' wrote Sir Kenneth Clark, and in the case of Robert Louis Stevenson, his childhood visions do seem to have been the main burden of the song.

As a child, Louis (as he was known to his family) would love nothing better than to walk from his city home down 'the wide thoroughfare that joins the city of my childhood [Edinburgh] with the sea,' to Leith harbour, where he would stand and stare at the great ships, and listen to the song of sailors as they pulled upon their ropes. 'In those days,' he recalled, 'I loved a ship as a man loves Burgundy or daybreak.'

There never was a seafaring adventure for boys before 'Treasure Island', and maybe none to match it since, nor does Louis' other adventure classic, 'Kidnapped', set in the aftermath of Culloden and drawing its power from historical fact coloured by romantic Jacobite legend, seem any less supportive of Clark's theory.

For, from the age of five, Louis accompanied his family on holiday from Lowland Edinburgh to the Bridge of Allen, gateway to the Scottish Highlands, near where the Jacobite adventurer Rob Roy held sway less than 100 years earlier. In the 1850s, Bridge of Allen was still a place bristling with daredevil atmosphere and swashbuckling anecdote, and Louis thrilled to stories of Highland derring-do told him by his father's friends.

The budding adventure writer drew inspiration, too, from true-life tales of danger and rescue recounted by his father about his own famous family of lighthouse engineers. 'My name is well known as that of the Duke of Argyle among the skippers and the seamen of my native land. There is scarce a deep sea light from the Isle of Man north about Berwick, but one of my blood designed it.' One had even helped smuggle Jacobites to France after the 1715 uprising.

True-life tales outdid even the excitement of the 'land of story-books' which, as an intelligent, only child, Louis inhabited as often as possible from the age of seven: 'Give me a highwayman and I was full to the brim; a Jacobite would do, but the highwayman was my favourite dish. I can still hear the merry clatter of the hoofs along the moonlit lane; night and the coming of day are still related in my mind with the doings of John Rann or Jerry Abershaw; and the words "post-chaise", "the Great North Road", "ostler" and "nag" still sound in my ear like poetry.'

A spirit of adventure so infused the young boy's mind that he came to believe that 'parts of me have seen life, and met adventures and sometimes met them well', and this in spite of (or perhaps because of) the consumptive reality.

As a youngster, Louis was laid low by chronic bronchial problems that frequently confined him to the 'land of counterpane', and would later exclude him from the family business and lead sadly to an early death at forty-four. It was characteristic of his fortitude, and revealing of the moral dimension which so many critics have overlooked in his adult writing, that Louis clung to the belief that 'our conscious years are but a moment in the history that builds us up'.

Back in the nursery, helping stir the genetic brew and adding her own ingredients culled from Calvinism, was little Louis' nanny, Alison Cunningham. The boy's illness placed him at her mercy, and it was in her charge that the darker wings of Louis' fancy first took flight.

Here the seeds were sown of ideas to take root later in 'The Strange Case of Dr Jekyll and Mr Hyde'. Violent fits of coughing and sickness would keep him awake long into the night, and Cummy, as he called her adoringly, 'would lift me out of bed and take me, rolled in blankets, to the window'. Looking out, together, across the starlit Firth of Forth, Cummy would administer her daily dose of terror which caused hideous nightmares and shocked Louis' mother when she found out what had been going on.

'I had an extraordinary terror of hell implanted in me by my good nurse, which used to haunt me terribly on stormy nights,' he recalled. 'It is to my nurse that I owe my high-strung religious ecstasies and terrors . . . I would not only lie awake to weep for Jesus, which I have done many a time, but I would fear to trust myself to slumber lest I was not accepted or should slip ere I awoke into eternal ruin. I remember repeatedly . . . waking from a dream of Hell, clinging to the horizontal bar of the bed, with my knees and chin together, my soul shaken, my body convulsed with agony.'

When boy turned man and realised his gift as storyteller he would reject the straight-jacket of Calvinism and emerge a free man, opposed to any ideology that threatened to imprison man's natural spirit, espousing instead a transcendental reality rooted in the mythic spirit of the heroic Highland landscape he so loved and

'The smell of water rising from all round . . . the sound of water everywhere . . . the birds on every bush and from every corner of the overhanging woods pealing out their notes until the air throbbed with them; and in the midst of this, the manse.'

from which, tragically, his sickness finally exiled him.

But the key to Louis' emotional and physical survival of his childhood and to the development of his rich imagination that engaged and acted upon the sights and sounds of his childhood, lies not in anything that happened to him in the city of his birth, but in the regular and long periods of recuperation from his illness which he spent in the countryside, in his grandfather's manse house in the Pentland Hills – periods which enabled the boy to express 'the unnatural activity of my mind'.

It is fruitless to say that Louis' illness made him a writer. He may have been a writer even had illness not prevented his becoming a lighthouse engineer. It is hard to believe that such an imagination as his would have remained unexpressed if he had been fit. Nevertheless, it was his illness that brought him time and time again into the magic environment of the house, and in particular the garden, of George Balfour, Minister of Colinton. And it was here, often alone, that Louis created his own world of dreams and played to the extraordinary accompaniment of his developing imagination.

It was a place in that time like no other: the garden cut into provinces by a great hedge of beech, and overlooked by the church and the terrace of the churchyard, where the tombstones were thick, and after nightfall 'spunkies' might be seen to dance, at least by children; flower-pots lying warm in sunshine's laurels and the great yew making elsewhere a pleasing shade; the smell of water rising from all round, with an added tang of paper-mills; the sound of water everywhere, and the sound of mills – the wheel and the dam singing their alternative strain; the birds on every bush and from every corner of the overhanging woods pealing out their notes until the air throbbed with them; and in the midst of this, the manse.

Colinton is no longer a little country village, it's a suburb of Edinburgh accessible by means of the City Ring Road. But once inside the manse you are in a timeless zone. It is important to appreciate the topography.

The site is enclosed on three sides by the graveyard of the church ('the terrace of the churchyard'), which is at certain points ten feet or more higher than the manse garden, so there is a sense of climbing down into a secret place. On the fourth side Leith Water courses beneath a steep high hill of trees reaching to the sky, which confirms the sense of seclusion. There is no sound other than the rush of water and the song of birds. The house itself is set more or less centrally in the garden, which gives four separate sections or provinces to the garden immediately. It is exactly as Louis described. Cut off from the outside world, a little world as private as the world of a child's mind, and just waiting to share its stories.

I was an only child and, it may be in consequence, both intelligent and sickly. I have three powerful impressions of my childhood: my sufferings when I was sick, my delights in convalescence at my grandfather's manse at Colinton, near Edinburgh, and the unnatural activity of my mind after I was in bed at night . . .

I have not space to tell of my pleasures at the manse. I have been happier since; for I think most people exaggerate the capacity for happiness of a child; but I have never again been happy in the same way. For indeed it was scarce a happiness of this world, as we conceive it when we are grown up, and was more akin to that of animal than to that of a man. The sense of sunshine, of green leaves, and the singing of birds, seems never to have been so strong in me as in that place. The deodar upon the lawn, the laurel thickets, the mills, the river, the church bell, the sight of people ploughing, the Indian curiosities with which my uncles had stocked the house, the

sharp contrast between this place and the city where I spent the other portion of my time, all these took hold of me, and still remain upon my memory, with a peculiar sparkle and sensuous excitement . . .

'Here is the weir with the wonder of foam.'

It is odd, after so long an interval, to recall these incidents that struck me deepest. Once, as I lay, playing hunter, hid in a thick laurel, and with a toy gun upon my arm, I worked myself so hotly into the spirit of my play, that I think I can still see the herd of antelope come sweeping down the lawn and round the deodar; it was almost a vision. Again, one warm summer evening on the front green, my aunt showed me the wing-bone of an albatross, told me of its largeness and how it slept upon the wing above the vast Pacific, and quote from the 'Ancient Mariner':

> *With my cross bow,*
> *I shot the Albatross.*

I do not believe anything so profoundly affected my imagination; and to this day, I am still faithful to the Albatross, as the most romantic creature of fable (or nature, I know not which), and the one, besides, that has the noblest name. I remember in particular, a view I had from an attic window, suddenly beholding, with delighted wonder, my ordinary playgrounds at my feet; and another outlook, when I climbed a hawthorn near the gate, and saw over the wall into the snuff-mill garden, thick with flowers and bright with sunshine, a paradise not hitherto expected.

The passage comes from an essay called 'Memories of Myself'.

There should be no disappointment in his having given no more information about 'my pleasures at the manse', because Louis painted their colours clearly when he celebrated both manse and garden in his book, 'A Child's Garden of Verses'.

In 'Keepsake Mill' we sense the natural rhythms of the place. The actual mill is now broken down, but all else remains – the river, the weir, even the 'breach in the wall':

> Over the borders, a sin without pardon,
> Breaking the branches and crawling below,
> Out through the breach in the wall of the garden,
> Down by the banks of the river we go.
>
> Here is the mill with the humming of thunder,
> Here is the weir with the wonder of foam,
> Here is the sluice with the race running under –
> Marvellous places, though handy to home.

Louis was a little shy about the verses: 'These are rhymes, jingles; I don't go in for eternity and the three unities,' he wrote to his biographer, the critic Sir Sidney Colvin. But deep down he knew what he had done. 'They seem to me to smile, to have a kind of childish treble note that sounds in my ears freshly – not song, if you will, but a child's voice,' he conceded in a letter to his friend Edmund Grosse.

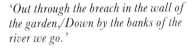

'Out through the breach in the wall of the garden,/Down by the banks of the river we go.'

Here, at the manse, Louis' aloneness is fun; first he meets his shadow –

I have a little shadow that goes in and out with me,
And what can be the use of him is more than I can see . . .

And then in comes the 'unseen playmate' of every only child –

When children are playing alone on the green,
In comes the playmate that never was seen . . .

He loves to be little, he hates to be big,
'Tis he that inhabits the caves that you dig;
'Tis he when you play with your soldiers of tin
That sides with the Frenchmen and never can win.

His garden is the 'land of story-books' come true. No longer does he just imagine, now he can become 'the leader of a great horde of irregular cavalry . . . turning in the saddle to look back at my whole command (some 5,000 strong) following me at the hard gallop up the road out of the burning valley by moonlight.' At Colinton (at last!) Louis can –

. . . play at books that I have read
Till it is time to go to bed.

Wars, maps, battles, kingdoms won and lost characterise his games. And even though, occasionally, he may fall sick, at the manse he transforms the dreaded 'land of counterpane':

And sometimes sent my ships in fleets
All up and down among the sheets;
Or brought my trees and houses out,
And planted cities all about.

In 'Historical Associations' the adult catches a glimpse of the garden through the eyes, through the mind, of the child he once was. It is no mere memory.

Dear Uncle Jim, this garden ground
That now you smoke your pipe around
Has seen immortal actions done
And valiant battles lost and won.

Here we had best on tip-toe tread,
While I for safety march ahead,
For this is that enchanted ground
Where all who loiter slumber sound.

Sydney Smith once said, 'If you make children happy, you will make them happy twenty years after by the memory of it.' The manse garden is still a playground, and the minister, George Whyte, does not wish to turn it into a museum. It is a playground for his two sons and open to the public only for parish functions. All is, however, being carefully preserved as it was in Stevenson's day.

Here is the sea, here is the sand,
Here is the simple Shepherd's Land,
Here are the fairy hollyhocks,
And there are Ali Baba's rocks.

But yonder, see! apart and high,
Frozen Siberia lies; where I,
With Robert Bruce and William Tell,
Was bound by an enchanter's spell.

There, then, awhile in chains we lay,
In wintry dungeons, far from day;
But ris'n at length, with might and main,
Our iron fetters burst in twain,

Then all the horns were blown in town;
And, to the ramparts clanging down,
All the giants leaped to horse
And charged behind us through the gorse.

On we rode, the others and I,
Over the mountains blue, and by
The Silent River, the sounding sea,
And the robber woods of Tartary.

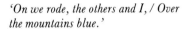

'On we rode, the others and I, / Over the mountains blue.'

A thousand miles we galloped fast,
And down the witches' lane we passed,
And rode amain, with brandished sword,
Up to the middle, through the ford.

Last we drew rein – a weary three –
Upon the lawn, in time for tea,
And from our steeds alighted down
Before the gates of Babylon.

The witches' lane, leading to the 'breach in the wall by the garden'.

He wrote the verses away from Colinton. Louis wrote best about a place when not in sight of it. He needed distance before his unconscious could go to work. (How important became his exile from Scotland through illness.) In the excerpt from 'To Minnie' (a poem named after his cousin Minnie, with whom he once visited India by climbing on a chair and beholding in awe a cabinet collection of Oriental 'bangles, beads and screens'), he returns in person to the manse garden. There is melancholy because Louis knows that he can no longer gain access through the gates of Babylon, the sacred city. No longer a child, he cannot hear the music right.

To Minnie
. . . the old manse is changed to-day;
It wears an altered face
And shields a stranger race.
The river, on from mill to mill,
Flows past our childhood's garden still;
But ah! we children never more
Shall watch it from the water-door!
Below the yew – it still is there –
Our phantom voices haunt the air
As we were still at play,
And I can hear them call and say:
'How far is it to Babylon?'

Ah, far enough, my dear,
Far, far enough from here –
Yet you have farther gone!
'Can I get there by candlelight?'
So goes the old refrain.
I do not know – perchance you might –
But only children hear it right,
Ah, never to return again!
The eternal dawn, beyond a doubt,
Shall break on hill and plain,
And put all stars and candles out,
Ere we be young again . . .

'How do you like to go up in a swing, / Up in the air so blue?' Here, under the spreading branches of the yew, Louis played at pirates. His swing was away being restored.

Arthur Ransome

b. 1884

*'No matter where I was, wandering about the world, I used at night to look
for the North Star and, in my mind's eye, could see the beloved skyline of
great hills beneath it. Swallows and Amazons grew out of those old memories.
I could not help writing it. It almost wrote itself.'*

Arthur Ransome was born on January 18th, 1884, in Leeds, where
his father was employed as Professor of History at the Yorkshire
Academy (later Leeds University).

Ransome tells us in his autobiography that he was something of
a disappointment to his parents; from an early age he manifested –
with a special intensity reserved for his father – what he called 'an
ineradicable tendency to disagree with any majority wherever I
happened to be'. Whatever his father's passions, from academic
work, to week-end country sports, to politics, Arthur would refuse
stubbornly to fall in line, even on one occasion (as a very small
boy) buying and wearing at the dinner-table the yellow elec-
tioneering rosette of Gladstone's party, simply because he knew
that 'my father loathed Mr Gladstone and all his works.'
Scholastically (Arthur went to Rugby) he was a particular
disappointment, and by the time he went out into the world he
had a strong sense from his father that he was heading for failure.
Nevertheless, there was no malice, no familial disharmony
between these two independent spirits, and in one significant
matter they were very much in accord.

Arthur's father had been born on the shores of Morecambe Bay,
at the southern edge of the Lake District, and held himself an
exile, even harbouring guilt at bringing up his four children in an
urban environment. As a result, most week-ends he would take
himself off to the hills to fish or to shoot, and at the earliest
opportunity ceremoniously offered up his firstborn to the spirit of
the fells: 'To make up as far as he could for his eldest son's being
born in a town, (he) carried me up to the top of Coniston Old Man
at such an early age that I think no younger human being can ever
have been there.'

Arthur Ransome's later enthusiasm and nostalgia for the Lake
District which characterise the five best-loved childrens books set
in and around the 'Lake in the North', owe everything to this early
initiation and its annual renewal.

Looking across the lake to Coniston Old Man.

I have been often asked how I came to write 'Swallows and Amazons'. The answer is that it had its beginning long, long ago when, as children, my brother, my sisters and I spent most of our holidays on a farm at the south end of Coniston . . . We adored the place . . . While away from it, as children and as grown-ups, we dreamt about it. No matter where I was, wandering about the world, I used at night to look for the North Star and, in my mind's eye, could see the beloved skyline of great hills beneath it. 'Swallows and Amazons' grew out of those old memories. I could not help writing it. It almost wrote itself.

During every Long Vacation the family took itself off, lock, stock and barrel, to the Lakes. Preparations began well before the end of term:

There would be an orgy of fly-tying. My father tied for his friends and for himself the delicate Yorkshire wet flies that T. E. Pritt pictured in his famous book, lightly hackled and dressed on short lengths of fine gut or horsehair. My father was one of the first to introduce Halford's methods in the North and to fish with dry fly, but after a year or so he gave up tying dry flies because he had no time to spare for them and he was himself first of all a wet-fly trout-fisher. Long before the day of the journey the wooden candlesticks in his study were festooned with new-made casts, his rods were ready, his landing-net mended, an inspection held of our perch-floats, and our shotted casts for perch-fishing hung beside his own. Meanwhile my mother was busy day after day patching and mending our clothes, replacing used half-pans of water-colour (she used to run short of cobalt blue) and buying (we used to remind her) sheets of transfers to keep us happy on the rainy days that we knew, in the Lake District, to be inevitable. A huge supply of ginger-nuts was bought for the train journey. At last came the great moment of Sitting on the Bath. The bath was a large, deep, tin one, painted a mottled orange-brown. It had a flat lid, a staple, a padlock and a huge leather strap over all. The bath, used at Christmas for a bran-pie, stuffed with presents, with a cotton-wool crust that was cut with a monster paper-knife, was now crammed with bedding and clothes that filled it and rose high above it. The lid was pressed down on the top and my mother began to wonder what could be left out. We children climbed on and slid off and climbed again. With the weight of all of us together the lid sank but never far enough. The end of the strap (which at first would not reach so far) was put through its buckle, and mother and nurse gained on it, one hole at a time. Still, blankets, sheets and underclothes oozed from beneath it and we went officiously about it and about, poking them back. Then, when we had done our utmost one of us was sent down for the cook, a big, cheerful, brawny Armstrong from Northumberland who allowed us in the kitchen but once a year, to wish while we stirred her Christmas pudding with a long-handled spoon, her own huge hands engulfing our small ones and providing the force to drive the spoon round and round through the stiff, currant-spotted mass of uncooked pudding. The cook would wipe her vast forearms, come up to the nursery, laugh at the sight of us waiting, defeated, round the bath, seat herself solidly on the lid and another half-dozen holes

Greenodd, where the Crake and the Leven pour together into the sea.

were gained in a moment. But even with the weight of Molly Armstrong I can never remember the lid closing far enough to let my mother use the padlock. 'It'll have to do now,' she would say, and that was that.

The next day there was a hurried run round to say farewell to the hole in the grubby evergreens (Leeds was a smoky city) that only we knew was a robbers' cave. Then came the drive down into Leeds in an old four-wheeled cab, the bulk of the luggage having gone before. The railway journey through the outskirts of Leeds, through smoky Holbeck, past the level crossing that we knew from our 'walks', and on by Wharfedale to Hellifield, my father's gun and rods on the rack, ginger-nuts crunching in our mouths, noses pressed to the windows to watch the dizzying rise and fall of the telegraph wires beside the track, was a long-drawn-out ecstasy, and not for children alone. By the time we reached Arkholme we could feel my father's mounting excitement (he had been pointing out to us one by one the rivers we crossed). At Carnforth we had to change from one train to another unless, as in later years, my father had been able to book an entire 'saloon' carriage for us and our luggage, so that we could sit in it until it was coupled to the other train, on the Furness Railway that we always counted as peculiarly our own. There were well-known landmarks as the train ran slowly round Morecambe Bay. There was the farmhouse that was built like a little fortress against raiding Scots. There was Arnside Tower. There were our own Lake hills, and Coniston Old Man with a profile very different from the lofty cone it showed to us at Nibthwaite. Then at last we were at Greenodd, where the Crake and the Leven poured together to the sea not a stone's throw from the railway line. There would be John Swainson from Nibthwaite, or Edward his son, with a red farmcart and a well beloved young lad with a wagonette. We climbed, or were lifted, down to the platform to be greeted by my father's old friend, the station-master, with the latest news of the two rivers. We watched the train go on without us across the bridge and away up the valley of the Leven. Anxiously we watched the loading of the cart, holding our breaths lest the bath should burst its strap before being roped down on the top of all. Then came the slow drive up the valley of the Crake,   always halting at the Thurstonville Lodge for a word

'Then came the slow drive up the valley of the Crake, always halting at the Thurstonville Lodge for a word with the keeper there.'

with the keeper there. Up the winding hill and down again by Lowick Green, over the river at Lowick Bridge, where my father had a look at that streamy water just below, as I have so often had a look sixty years later. We stopped again by a little wooden bridge close to one of my father's favourite places, and again by the Hart Jackson's cottage, had a glimpse of Allan Tarn, rumbled over Nibthwaite Beck at the entrance to the tiny village, turned to the right up the road to Bethecar, a steep short pull between barn and orchard, for which we all got out, and there we were at the farm, being greeted by Mrs Swainson and her daughters, and getting our first proper sight of the lake itself – Coniston Water.

Tea was always ready for our arrival, and after the long journey we were always made to get that meal over before doing anything else. Then 'May I get down?' and we were free in paradise, sniffing remembered smells as we ran about making sure that familiar things were still in their places. I used first of all to race down to the lake, to the old stone harbour to which, before the Furness Railways built its branch line to Coniston village, boats used to bring their cargoes of copper-ore from the mines on the Old Man. The harbour was a rough stone-built dock, with an old shed or two, and beside it was a shallow cut, perhaps six feet across and twenty long, where the Swainson's boat, *our* boat, was pulled up half way out of the shallow, clear water which always seemed alive with minnows. I had a private rite to

'Up the winding hill and down again by Lowick Green, over the river at Lowick Bridge, where my father had a look at the streamy water just below.'

perform. Without letting the others know what I was doing, I had to dip my hand in the water, as a greeting to the beloved lake or as a proof to myself that I had indeed come home. In later years, even as an old man, I have laughed at myself, resolved not to do it, and every time have done it again. If I were able to go back there today, I should feel some discomfort until coming to the shore of the lake I had felt its coolness on my fingers.

After the solemn secret touching of the lake I had to make sure that other things were as they had been. I used to race back to the farmhouse, to find my father already gone with a rod to the river, my mother and our nurse

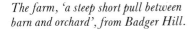

The farm, 'a steep short pull between barn and orchard', from Badger Hill.

busy unpacking, and (though the younger ones might be detained) nothing wanted from me except to keep out of the way. I had to make sure that the butter-churn was in its old place, and the grandfather clock in the kitchen still whirring wheezily as it struck the hours. I had to glance into the earth closet in the garden, with its three sociable seats, two for grown-ups and one small one for a baby in the middle, to see that there had been no change in the decoration of its walls. These were papered with pages from *Punch* bearing the mystic word 'charivari' and with pictures from the *Illustrated London News*, including portraits of Mr Gladstone, of whom (after the affair of the yellow ribbon) I was an obstinate supporter. The newspapers, no doubt, had been left by other visitors, and the pictures showing Conservatives and Liberals alike impartially pasted up by the farmer.

Those holidays at Nibthwaite I owe to my father's passion for the lake country. They bred a similar passion in me that has lasted my life and been the mainspring of the books I have been happiest in writing. Always that country has been 'home', and smoky old Leeds, though well beloved, was never as real as Swainson's farm, Coniston lake and the valley of the Crake. There, in the heavy farm boat, with its oars that worked on pins instead of in row-locks (so that a fisherman could drop them instantly if a pike or a char took his trailed spinner) I learned to be at home on the water.

There was no end to the pleasures of Nibthwaite. We made friends with

Looking down towards the old stone harbour where 'the Swainson's boat, our boat, was pulled up' and where, every year Ransome had an important private rite to perform.

The children establish their camp on Wild Cat Island and meet the strange charcoal burners and their captive adder, just as Ransome did when he was a boy.

the farm animals, with the charcoal-burners who in those days still dwelt in wigwams carefully watching their smoking mounds, with the postman, several gamekeepers, several poachers and various fishermen. We took part in the haymaking, turned the butter-churn for Annie Swainson, picked mushrooms and blackberries, tickled trout under the little bridge, went for rare educative walks with my father who, like my grandfather, was a first-rate ornithologist and naturalist (though neither he nor my mother was good on the names of wild flowers). That road along the east side of Coniston lake, now dangerous with motor traffic, was then very little used. I came once upon a red squirrel, rolled up in a ball, fast asleep on a sunny patch in the middle of the road, picked it up to put it in safety and was well bitten for my pains. I also came upon a wounded heron and, knowing no better, took it in my arms and carried it back to Nibthwaite, looking for first aid. I was lucky not to lose an eye. The heron kept stabbing with its long bill, and I suppose I escaped only because I was holding my patient so tight in my arms that with its head at my shoulder it could not reach my face.

We used to catch minnows in the little cut where the Swainsons kept their boat, and we were taken perch-fishing, each of us watching a float of a different colour. This, of course, was very different from merely watching someone else catch fish. Then too sometimes, when my father was fishing the lake for trout he would row his whole family up to Peel Island where we landed in the lovely little harbour at the south end (that some who have read my books as children may recognise borrowed for the sake of secrecy to improve an island in another lake). We spent the day as savages. My mother would settle down to make a sketch in water-colours. My father, forgetting to eat his sandwiches, would drift far along the lake-shores, casting his flies and coming back in the evening with trout in the bottom of the boat for Mrs

'Then too, sometimes, when my father was fishing the lake for trout he would row his whole family up to Peel Island where we landed in the lovely little harbour at the south end.'

Readers of Swallows and Amazons *will recognise the little harbour at Peel Island as that of Wild Cat Island, where the Swallows camp out.*

Swainson to cook for next day's breakfast.

Once out of school, Ransome developed an extraordinary desire to educate himself and succeed in spite of his family's earlier despair. He first worked in London as an office boy for a publisher, before graduating to ghost-writing and reviewing. By the age of twenty he had produced a book of essays, his first book under his own name – not bad for someone who had felt a failure at school.

All the while the Lake District had continued to exert its influence. In William Holmes of Ulverston, he found a publisher for his essays, but more significantly, during his first trip to the Lakes after leaving Rugby he met by chance W G Collingwood, who besides being Ruskin's biographer happened to be the author of the legendary 'Thorstein of the Mere', a book about the coming of the Norsemen to Coniston (for long called Thurstonwater) – 'the best-loved book of my boyhood'.

They got on and Collingwood invited him to his house. Ransome chose the first full day of a working holiday the following year to take up the invitation which signalled the beginning of a new formative period, a sort of second childhood in which Collingwood and his family provided what had been missing in the first.

That first day Mr Collingwood, though he was at work when I came, took me into his study. I can see it now, the books from floor to ceiling, the enormous long table piled with books and manuscripts, the unfinished canvas on an easel, the small table at which he was writing and, over the fireplace, his lovely portrait of his wife, in a small boat with two of the children. He put me in one arm-chair, shifted his from the table and asked about what I was doing. The miracle for me was his assumption that what I was trying to do was worth doing. Later in the morning room I met Mrs Collingwood who was soon, when he spoke of her to me, to become 'your aunt', the Dorrie to whom on one of her birthdays Ruskin had lifted his glass with the toast, 'To Dorrie – and all angels!' The two elder girls (the youngest was away at school) came in with their painting things from the garden, and with them an Austrian cousin, very voluble in an English entirely her own. Dora was a year and Barbara two years younger than myself, Hilde, the cousin, about the same age. In the afternoon we went down to their boathouse and out in the *Swallow*, a one-time fishing-boat, monstrously heavy to row but not bad under sail, the first of a long dynasty of *Swallows* in my sailing life. I came back with them to supper and walked round the head of the lake to my lodgings with my head in a whirl, now and then skipping in the happy privacy of the dark. A new life had begun for me that day. From that day Mr and Mrs Collingwood treated me as a son of their own. From that day I had behind me a family who did not assume that I was heading for some disastrous failure and were not convinced that whatever I was doing I should be better employed doing something else. Those two gave me something I had not missed because I had not till then known that it could be. The whole of the rest of my life has been happier because of them.

Next day I was on the lake again with the three girls. We rowed to Lands Point where, while I lay on the shore and wrote, they made sketches of the old Hall of the le Flemings and its boathouse, and I remember that as we rowed away Hilde made us turn back. There was a white lifebelt hanging on the wall of the boathouse and Hilde noticed it only as we were rowing out of the bay. 'Quick!' she cried. 'One other minute! I have forgot the safety circle.' I was bidden to come early next morning and 'my aunt' packed us off with a bun-loaf, a pot of marmalade and a kettle to go down the lake to Peel Island, the island that had mattered so much to me as a small boy, was in the distant future to play its part in some of my books, and is still, in my old age, a crystallising point for happy memories.

Some twenty-five years were to pass before Ransome published the first of his classic adventure stories for children, 'Swallows and Amazons'.

In the interim he had travelled to Russia to learn the language, covered the Revolution for the Daily News, married Trotsky's secretary, Evgenia Shelepin, and returned to England, settling in the Winster Valley to the east of Lake Windermere.

Taking up his friendship with Barbara Collingwood, by then settled with a family of her own at Bank Ground, he and Barbara's husband, Ernest Altounyan, taught their children – Taqui, Susan, Titty, Roger and Brigit – to sail in two dinghies – *Swallow* (Ransome's boat), and *Mavis*.

During that glorious summer of 1928, in the process of sharing with his young charges the spirit of his own youth, long-gone, Ransome began to cast his impressions in lasting fictional form.

In the Preface to Ransome's 'Autobiography', Sir Rupert Hart-Davis pays tribute to the realism of 'Swallows and Amazons' – 'Of all the questions that his young readers asked him, one was prominant and recurring – the question, "Is it real?" . . . And with this question they touched the heart of Ransome's secret.'

The novel which gives its name to his classic series is the story of two sailing dinghies – *Swallow* and *Amazon* (definitely an improvement on *Mavis*), one occupied by John, Susan, Titty and Roger (the Swallows), and the other by the piratical Amazons, 'Nancy and Peggy, who had sprung to life one day when, sailing on Coniston, I had seen two girls playing on the lake-shore.'

The Swallows camp out on Wild Cat Island (a composite of Peel Island on Coniston and Blakeholme on Windermere) while their mother stays at Holly Howe on the mainland (Bank Ground). Day-to-day duties are assigned, an ideal secret harbour (similar to a natural harbour on Peel Island) is found for their boat, and the strange charcoal burners, a family that had plied its trade on the otherwise deserted island for a hundred years, and first met by Ransome as a boy, make an appearance with their captive adder. There is the sailing and the fishing and the swimming and the altercations with Captain Flint and his parrot on the Captain's houseboat moored in Houseboat Bay – the Gondola of Ransome's childhood, today still touring Coniston. And finally there are the piratical exploits of the Amazons and counter-strategies by the Swallows.

He had the whole story clear in his head, but approached its writing with caution: 'I had only to write it, but dreaded the discovery after all these years of writing discursively I was unable to write narrative. I well remember the pleasure I had in the first chapter, and my fear that it would also be the last. I could think of nothing else, and grudged every moment that had to be given to other activities.'

Perhaps, besides reservations about his technical skill as story-teller, his initial anxiety harboured a sense of humility that he had come upon the means to express a moment so precious to him, the moment of childhood held in imagination so long and always tantalisingly out of reach.

His pleasure in realising its expression is ours – the child shines through.

L P Hartley

b. 1895

'Certain moments in the past were like buried treasure to Eustace, living relics of a golden age which it was an ecstacy to contemplate. His toys put him in touch with these secret jewels of experience . . .'
from 'The Shrimp and the Anemone'

Leslie Poles Hartley was born in 1895 at Whittlesea between Peterborough and March, the second child of an up-and-coming country solicitor.

When Leslie was five and Enid, his elder sister, was eight, the family moved nearer to Peterborough and took a larger house. Fletton Tower, as the house was called (aptly, for its new owner would later make a success out of a third-share he took in a local brickworks), was in the gift of a wealthy land speculator, who had bought the surrounding area to develop and was a client of Leslie's father.

Here, three years later, in 1903, Norah Hartley was born, and dwells today, a world authority on staghounds and perhaps the last person able to shed reliable light, of a biographical nature, on one of this country's most important but private 20th-century literary figures.

'The Shrimp and the Anemone', Hartley's first novel and the initial book of a trilogy known by the title of its ultimate volume, 'Eustace and Hilda', tells the story of a summer holiday spent by the boy Eustace and his sister at a seaside resort called Anchorstone.

'The Shrimp' is remarkable for its insight into the emotional life of the two siblings and its meticulously observed detail of child play. After reading the novel, no parent could watch its children playing on the beach in quite the same way again.

In the build-up to the passage excerpted below, his younger sister Barbara's possessiveness over toys that belong to Eustace has led him to assert right-of-ownership over a toy rabbit, which earns him a rebuke from the adults for being mean. Hilda, turning the knife in Eustace's wound, urges that he be sent to bed for his sins – 'It will be good for him in the end.'

Eustace becomes violent.

On the beach, in the cool light of day, Eustace realises that he must apologise to Hilda, set matters straight – 'It was understood that from their private disputes there was no appeal to a disinterested tribunal.'

Fletton Tower near Peterborough

Their seaside games are as seriously absorbing as Ransome's or Stevenson's but loaded with emotional content and barbed with symbolism, as Hilda, mercilessly, lethally, reasserts her dominant position in a world wholly the children's own.

I needed to know how much of it was true. Could Leslie really have suffered so, at the hands of a real elder sister? The sheer power of the writing seemed to insist upon it. Miss Norah Hartley agreed to see me. I went warily. Perhaps Hilda's blood ran in the family.

Enid and Leslie; Hilda and Eustace?

There she sat, on the large rock in their pond which they had christened Gibraltar, her back bent, her legs spread out, her head drooping. It was an ugly attitude and she would grow like that, thought Eustace uncomfortably. Moreover she was sitting recklessly on the wet seaweed which would leave a green mark and give her a cold, if salt water could give one a cold . . . Still Hilda did not move. Her distress conveyed itself to him across the intervening sand. He glanced uneasily at Nancy who was constructing a garden out of seaweed and white pebbles at the gateway of the castle – an incongruous adjunct, Eustace thought, for it was precisely there that the foemen would attack.

He had almost asked her to put it at the back, for the besieged to retire into in their occupied moments; where it was it spoilt his vision of the completed work and even sapped his energy. But he did not like the responsibility of interfering and making people do things his way. He worked on, trying to put Hilda out of his mind, but she recurred and at last he said: 'I think I'll go back now, if it's all the same to you.'

He hoped by this rather magnificent phrase to make his departure seem as casual as possible, but Nancy saw through him.

'Can't leave your big sister?' she inquired, an edge of irony in her voice. 'She'll get over it quicker if you let her alone.'

Eustace declined this challenge. It pained him to think that his disagreement with Hilda was public property.

'Oh, she's all right now,' he told Nancy airily. 'She's having a rest.'

'Well, give her my love,' said Nancy.

Eustace felt a sudden doubt, from her tone, whether she really meant him to deliver the message. . .

It was too bad of Hilda to leave his hat lying in a pool. However cross she might be she rarely failed to retrieve his personal belongings over which, even when not flustered and put out, he had little control. Now the ribbon was wet and the '*table*' of 'Indomi*table*', a ship which he obscurely felt he might be called upon at any moment to join, stood out more boldly than the rest. Never mind, it was salt-water, and in future the hat could be used for a barometer, like seaweed, to tell whether bad weather was coming. Meanwhile there was Hilda. It was no good putting off the evil moment: she must be faced.

But he did not go to her at once. He dallied among the knee-high rocks for which the beach at Anchorstone was famous. He even built a small, almost vertical castle, resembling, as nearly as he could make it, the cone of

Cotopaxi, for which he had a romantic affection, as he had for all volcanoes, earthquakes and violent manifestations of Nature. He calculated the range of the lava flow, marking it out with a spade and contentedly naming for destruction the various capital cities, represented by greater and lesser stones, that fell within its general circumference. In his progress he conceived himself to be the Angel of Death, a delicious pretence, for it involved flying and the exercise of supernatural powers. On he flew. Could Lisbon be destroyed a second time? It would be a pity to waste the energy of the eruption on what was already a ruin; but no doubt they had rebuilt it by now. Over it went, and in addition, an enormous tidal wave swept up the Tagus, ravaging the interior. The inundation stopped at Hilda's feet. . .

'It only just missed you,' he remarked cryptically.

Silence.

'You only just escaped; it was a narrow shave,' Eustace persisted, still hoping to interest his sister in her deliverance.

'What fool's trick is this?' demanded Hilda in a far-away voice.

Discouraging as her words were, Eustace took heart; she was putting on her tragedy airs, and the worst was probably over.

'It was an eruption,' he explained, 'and you were the city of Athens and you were going to be destroyed. But they sacrificed ten Vestal Virgins for you and so you were saved.'

'What a silly game!' commented Hilda, her pose on the rock relenting somewhat. 'Did you learn it from Nancy?'

Out of season, the huge silent expanse of beach at Anchorstone gives the impression of having entombed not just Eustace's past beneath its shifting sands.

'Oh no,' said Eustace, 'we hardly talked at all – except just at the end, to say good-bye.'

Hilda seemed relieved to hear this.

'I don't know why you go and play with people if you don't talk to them,' she said. 'You wouldn't if you weren't a goose.'

'Oh, and Nancy sent you her love,' said Eustace.

'She can keep it,' said Hilda, rising from the rock, some of which, as Eustace had feared, came away with her. 'You've been very cruel to me, Eustace,' she went on. 'I don't think you really love me.'

Hilda never made a statement of this kind until the urgency of her wrath was past. Eustace also used it, but in the heat of his.

'I do love you,' he asserted.

'You don't love me.'

'I do.'

'You don't – and don't argue,' added Hilda crushingly. 'How can you say you love me when you leave me to play with Nancy?'

'I went on loving you all the time I was with Nancy,' declared Eustace almost in tears.

'Prove it!' cried Hilda.

To be nailed down to a question he couldn't answer gave Eustace a feeling of suffocation. The elapsing seconds seemed to draw the very life out of him.

'There!' exclaimed Hilda triumphantly. 'You can't!'

For a moment it seemed to Eustace that Hilda was right: since he couldn't prove that he loved her, it was plain he didn't love her. He became very despondent. But Hilda's spirits rose with her victory, and his own, more readily acted upon by example than by logic, caught the infection of hers. Side by side they walked round the pond and examined the damage. It was an artificial pond – a lake almost – lying between rocks. The intervals between the rocks were dammed up with stout banks of sand. To fill the pond they had to use borrowed water, and for this purpose they dug channels to the natural pools left by the tide at the base of the sea-wall. A network of conduits criss-crossed over the beach, all bringing their quota to the pond which grew deeper and deeper and needed ceaselessly watching. It was a morning's work to get the pond going properly, and rarely a day passed without the retaining wall, in spite of their utmost vigilance, giving way in one place or other. If the disaster occurred in Eustace's section, he came in for recrimination, if in Hilda's, she blamed herself no less vigorously, while he, as a rule, put in excuses for her which were ruthlessly and furiously set aside.

But there was no doubt that it was Hilda who kept the spirit of pond-making alive. Her fiery nature informed the whole business and made it exciting and dangerous. When anything went wrong there was a row – no clasping of hands, no appealing to Fate, no making the best of a bad job. Desultory, amateurish pond-making was practised by many of the Anchorstone children: their puny, half-hearted, untidy attempts were, in Hilda's eyes, a disgrace to the beach. Often, so little did they understand the pond-making spirit, they would wantonly break down their own wall for the pleasure of watching the water go cascading out. And if a passer-by mischievously trod on the bank they saw their work go to ruin without a

Eustace 'dallied among the knee-high rocks', but, alas, a storm twenty years ago shifted so much sand onto the beach from the sea that today they are all but buried.

sigh. But woe betide the stranger who, by accident or design, tampered with Hilda's rampart! Large or small, she gave them a piece of her mind; and Eustace, standing some way behind, balanced uncertainly on the edge of the conflict, would echo some of his sister's less provocative phrases, by way of underlining. When *their* wall gave way it was the signal for an outburst of frenzied activity. On one never forgotten day Hilda had waded knee-deep in the water and ordered Eustace to follow. To him this voluntary immersion seemed cataclysmic, the reversal of a lifetime's effort to keep dry. They were both punished for it when they got home.

The situation had been critical when Eustace, prospecting for further sources of supply, came upon the anemone on the rock; while he delayed, the pond burst, making a rent a yard wide and leaving a most imposing delta sketched with great ruinous curves in low relief upon the sand. The pond was empty and all the imprisoned water had made its way to the sea. Eustace secretly admired the out-rush of sand and was mentally transforming it into the Nile estuary at the moment when Hilda stuck her spade into it. Together they repaired the damage and with it the leison in their affections; a glow of reconciliation pervaded them, increasing with each spadeful. Soon the bank was as strong as before. But you could not help seeing there had been a catastrophe, for the spick-and-span insertion proclaimed its freshness, like a patch in an old suit. And for all their assiduous dredging of the channels the new supplies came down from the pools above in the thinnest trickle, hardly covering the bottom and leaving bare a number of small stones which at high water were decently submerged. They had no function except by the order of their disappearance to measure the depth of the pond; now they stood out, emblems of failure, noticeable for the first time, like a handful of conventional remarks exchanged between old friends when the life has gone out of their relationship.

Presently Hilda, who possessed a watch, announced that it was dinner time.

'My brother's memory for the events of his childhood was very clear,' said Norah Hartley when we met. 'But clearer still was his memory of their effect on his emotions.'

'Anchorstone is Hunstanton on the Wash. We went there for holidays, Enid and Leslie more than I. You see, I was so much younger. Leslie was eight years and Enid was eleven years older than me. I was very much alone. They were very nice to me always, but many of their enjoyments I couldn't take part in.

'He was drawing on his own childhood memories, but . . . Let me put it this way, my sister was very sweet to me, not in the least overwhelming; if I had been in Eustace's place, it would have been my *mother* that would have been the prototype . . .

'My mother . . . My mother was excessively nervous about health, almost paranoid on the subject of health. She was always worried, always frightened, chiefly for her health. That bothered my father – her nervous temperament – because he was not like

'It was Hilda who kept the spirit of pond-making alive. Her fiery nature informed the whole business and made it exciting and dangerous.'

that, he was very philosophical (if it happens, it happens). Also, generally, she got her way in things.

'We did not get on as well as I would have liked. She was very fidgety and I was easily upset and between the two . . . well, the nursery was rather a refuge. Enid was the buffer between my father and the curious attitude that my mother had to live. Later, Enid knew that if she married, my father's life would be much less happy, and I am sure that was why she didn't marry.

'But Leslie and mother. He was very fond of her, and it was reciprocated. But he found her affection a weight to carry. This is all too easy to do unfortunately to a child of which you are fond. If only she could have realised what a worry she was to him, but she couldn't see it. Later on, we tried to point it out, to encourage her to let go. But it was no good.

'It was something with which he had to contend. He realised that he wasn't going to have a life of his own unless he struck out for it. But he didn't want to strike out for it, because he was a very gentle and loving person, and didn't want to hurt his mother. He realised either he must give up his own life or else hurt my mother. That I think was a struggle that had to go on in him. And I think it did.'

Suddenly the dialogue on the beach between Eustace and Hilda took on a completely different hue. Eustace undeniably Leslie, but the boy's emotions, his desire to please, to make Hilda be happy, to assuage his own sense of guilt, and the impossibility of his ever really succeeding, became the cry of a child for a mother he loved but whose emotional needs he was ultimately incapable of satisfying. I didn't wonder that when Leslie grew up he recalled the effect upon the child's sensibility.

When Eustace and Hilda leave the beach for dinner, they pause for a while at the top of the cliffs by the 'Try-Your-Grip machine, and survey the sands below:

There lay the pond, occupying an area of which anyone might be proud, but – horrors! – it was completely dry. It could not have overflowed of itself, for they had left it only a quarter full. The gaping hole in the retaining wall must be the work of an enemy. A small figure was walking away from the scene of demolition with an air of elaborate unconcern. 'That's Gerald Steptoe,' said Hilda. 'I should like to kill him!'

'He's a very naughty boy, he doesn't pay any attention to Nancy,' remarked Eustace, hoping to mollify his sister.

'She's as bad as he is! I should like to –' Hilda looked around her, at the

Anchorstone is Hunstanton, with its famous red cliffs.

sky above and the sea beneath.

'What would you do?' asked Eustace fearfully.

'I should tie them together and throw them off the cliff!'

Eustace tried to conceal the pain he felt.

'Oh, but Nancy sent you her love!'

'She didn't mean it. Anyhow I don't want to be loved by her.'

'Who would you like to be loved by? asked Eustace.

Hilda considered. 'I should like to be loved by somebody great and good.'

'Well, I love you,' said Eustace.

'Oh, that doesn't count. You're only a little boy. And Daddy doesn't count, because he's my father so he has to love me. And Minney doesn't count, because she . . . she hasn't anyone else to love!'

'Barbara loves you,' said Eustace, trying to defend Hilda from her own gloomy conclusions. 'Look how you make her go to sleep when nobody else can.'

'That shows how silly you are,' said Hilda. 'You don't love people because they send you to sleep. Besides, Barbara is dreadfully selfish. She's more selfish than you were at her age.'

'Can you remember that?' asked Eustace timidly.

'Of course I can, but Minney says so too.'

'Well, Aunt Sarah?' suggested Eustace doubtfully. 'She's so good she must love us all – and specially you, because you're like a second mother to us.'

Hilda gave one of her loud laughs.

'She won't love you if you're late for dinner,' she said, and started at a great pace up the chalky footpath. Eustace followed more slowly, still searching his mind for a lover who should fulfil his sister's requirements. But he could think of no one but God or Jesus, and he didn't like to mention their names except in church or at his prayers or during Scripture lessons.

Chapter Five: *Lost Content*

That is the land of lost content,
I see it shining plain,
The happy highways where I went
And cannot come again.
A E Housman

Edmund Blunden

b. 1896

'Over there are faith, life, virtue in the sun.'

For a whole host of children born at the tail end of the 19th Century the First World War marked a terrible frontier between innocence and adult worldliness.

First-hand experience of the horror of war consigned blissful childhood visions to doubtful memory, and post-war technological and economic changes seemed set finally to dismantle an already crumbling rural culture, leaving much that was good behind.

As the historian A L Rowse put it, the war broke the continuity of ancient custom – 'The war brought all that life of habit to a sudden full stop, held it suspended, breathless for a full four years in the shadow of its wing, and meanwhile set in being motions and tendencies which came to full flood the moment the War was over and swept away the old landmarks in a tide of change. I remember the momentary return to the old ways, for we celebrated Armistice with a Flora Dance through the town. There was something instinctive, pathetic about it, like a gesture remembered from some former existence, which had no meaning any more . . . Not all the good will in the world could construct the fabric of the old ways; in the years immediately after the War, they vanished like snows touched by the sun, like a dream "remembered on waking".'

One of England's most gifted poets, seeing perhaps the cultural and spiritual consequences for the nation of unnaturally accelerated fundamental change, and at the same time trying to make sense of his own terrible war-time experience, sought to bring to mind – to his and ours – what at root really matters in life. Unsurprisingly, he turned to his pre-war childhood vision of the

Looking out from the church tower over the clustering oast houses of Yalding. 'I can fairly say, not forgetting those miseries which childhood only understands as miseries, that life was not so bad in that Kentish village before the war. . Slow? You might accuse us of being so, but we should have been puzzled and obstinate.'

village of Yalding in the Garden of England, his land of 'lost content'.

> O happiest village! how I turned to you
> Beyond estranging years that cloaked my view
> With all their heavy fogs of fear and strain;
> I turned to you, I never turned in vain . . .
>
> Then all about these vasty walls our play
> Would hold the evening's lanterned gloom at bay,
> And senses young received each new-found thing
> As meadows feel and glow with eager spring . . .
> *from 'Old Homes'*

In his memorial address to Edmund Blunden, Sir Rupert Hart-Davis said, 'It is interesting . . . to wonder whether he would have remained a purely pastoral poet if he and his generation had not been engulfed in tragedy.'

War was the fire in which this poet's pastoral vision was forged (a vision synonymous with childhood joy); he wished it wasn't so, but war was what gave it its keen edge.

From early on in Blunden's life, there is a sense of foreboding, of unease at what is to come.

The twelfth-century church with its multitude of graves and gravestones, its strong tower and far-resounding ring of bells, stood only a few steps from our garden gate. It did things to our imagination. I had to have bells of my own, and with Lottie's help I contrived them. She got me at need one of the dress-weights which lived with my mother's reels of thread and collection of buttons and beads; this became the clapper of my mighty bell, that is to say some carefully chosen tin can, lashed to a stick. The stick was fixed across twigs in a tree-top, so that the bell would swing correctly and could be pulled and rung; but what pleased me more was to wake in a night of gale and rain, and hear my bell clanking with odd rhythm though no hand was ringing it, except that of the wind. One such stormy night it was not that beloved tinkling noise I heard. The deep and ominous thumping of drums was in my ears as I started up on my pillow; it went on, and I was sure it came from the churchyard, from opening graves . . .

> Drummers jumping from the tombs
> Banged and thumped all through the town . . .
> *from 'Death of Childhood Beliefs'*

Among the 'multitude of gravestones' of the churchyard of St Peter and St Paul, whence the young Edmund heard a 'deep and ominous thumping of drums'.

Intimations of Armageddon? The drums of war? he prefers to think not. Though the image is repeated in more than one of his poems, he prefers a more down-to-earth explanation: 'The drumming which I mentioned before might have been the consequence of having stood behind Mr Longley at the verge of some new grave – my friend Maggie Parham's, for instance – while the grave-digger "stomped" the earth down upon the coffin.'

Edmund Blunden was a gifted poet and a fine scholar. Sir Rupert Hart-Davis recalls coming upon him in a train during a blackout in London and finding him peering at latin verses by the light of a pencil torch. There are poets who work over their own verses until they feel they are right. Blunden wrote his straight off and rarely made changes. There's a naturalness about them, which is all-convincing; no straining; his poems come, like truth, untampered. He was also a modest man, down-to-earth, so when he received visions like the drummers, which he seems often to have done, he accepted them and let them do their work without fuss or intervention, or even much surprise.

. . . One evening, lying wide awake although I had been packed off to sleep, I was gazing southward at the window and then at the infinite blue beyond 'The Elms'. Without any particular notion of anything out of the common, I saw there in the glowing sky a range of architecture; not quite 'A rose-red city, half as old as time,' for the fabric looked new, but a series of tall-many-windowed brick buildings. Some years afterwards, on first approaching the extensive buildings of the great school in Sussex to which I had the luck to go, I was oddly aware that the scene was not quite unknown to me. It had been mine by some mysterious order at our old home.

Still thinking of almost sixty years ago, I will not arrange too methodically what comes to light. Ours was a world of wonder, mixed with dull and common things. The older poets of England speak with some regard of the motes in the sunbeams. Well did I observe that marvel too. Playing with my ball on the stairs of our small house, I could often see the ray of light stream through the keyhole of the front door, and in it such populous throngs of tiny atoms tingling and dancing, bright to the eye but ever free of the catching hand.

Edmund's parents taught at the local school in Yalding and his father, Charles, was organist and choirmaster at the church.

When we were droning away in school on a fine morning, it was paradise to hear all round the crowing of cocks and clucking of hens, mooing of cows and cawing of rooks, and many other voices of content from yard and pasture. But there was also now and then the painful screeching of some unfortunate pig aware of his doom . . .

Out of school a little party of us, including Alfred and Alice Cheesman from Church Cottages, used to plan and perform important journeys into the Kintons. This was a wide stretch of meadow sloping down to a pretty river called the Beult. In it more than one place was famous. An old hawthorn at the top had roots like chairs, almost polished by sheep rubbing their fleeces against them. Towards the river, a big oak was sometimes accompanied by horse-mushrooms, all seeming of similar bigness. A shallow

The river Beult 'came deep and slow to the mill-dam . . . The real river went through a tall floodgate over a weir into a pool.'

of the river with a steep little headland over it was The Sands. This green region became my private elysium for some years. Here I came upon things which everyone knows but which, first encountered, changed the world: the glorious yellow flag-flower in the swampy hollow, the rabbits playing and racing by their sandy buries, the sorrel and dewberry and oak-apple (the little boys in those days did not miss celebrating Oak-Apple Day), and of course the minnow and fresh-water mussel and wasp-nest and war-painted dragon-fly. Mostly the children went in a party, and with the air of conspirators. It was an age of daisy-chains, and the buttercup game ('do you like butter?'), and sand-castles, and paddling – sometimes more . . .

The river Beult came deep and slow, with borders of willow and a kind of bamboo one side and meadow and maybush the other, to the mill-dam. There one stream was sent through a tunnel to the big mill-wheel and plunged into a dark shade whitened with its splashing, foaming life. The other stream, the real river, went through a tall floodgate over a weir into a pool which could not be seen from any road, but lay deep and round and broad with a thick copse and oak-trees sheltering its banks. Mill-tail and main stream joined after a short travel and between them formed an island of wilderness where thistles and tansies and ox-eye daisies flourished without correction. There was room for our play with bat and ball, but it was the waterside which we haunted most, and though the bullfinch and the dove often made music there it was the sound of the falling and the rippling waters which we chiefly heard.

About the pool itself fear and mystery dwelt; we had ideas of the tremendous depth of the abyss below the weir, and even Mr Baldock, who looked after the floodgates and the penstocks, spoke of that on a winter's night with a tone of awe. Besides, one day two well-known youths were drowned as they swam there . . .

The art of angling had grown on me, and I even kept a little book with dates, weights, and other records of my victims. It was my feeling and still is that fishing with too fine killing tackle is no sport, and I commonly got an old willow stem from the tangled wood at New Bridges and fished with that and the simplest of watercord, corks, and hooks . . . . One day Will Baldock was with me . . . and the game was slow. Cheveney chimes warned us home already. My line was some of that coloured wax thread which was or ought to have been used at the infants' school for some improving minor art. Looking into a deep hole which we seldom bothered about, under a knobbly willow stump, I saw what looked like a length of hop-pole in the shadows. I had a gudgeon ready as a bait and quietly put him in the water; the pike, for that was the pole-like shape beneath, swallowed him at once. I ventured to pull, and the pike at once snapped my line and moved. But he had to pass a shallow either way. By this time Will occupied one end and I waded into the other, but the pike shot past me still trailing a bit of pink cord and a float. We watched him by these along the stream, till we met two grown-ups fishing, and while we reported our adventure the pike appeared. 'So help me God he is a bloody fine fish,' said one of the anglers. It was like a bit of the Benedicite: in spite of the swear-word . . .

All Edmund Blunden's childhood memories seem to coalesce in an

There was 'fear and mystery' about the pool, 'one day two well-known youths were drowned as they swam there.'

The Beult, beyond the Kintons, in the region that became Edmund's 'private elysium for some years. Here I came upon things which everyone knows but which, first encountered, changed the world.'

image of the Church of St Peter and St Paul, which, in those far-off days, was a clear expression of unity and purpose in village life.

The church then and for years afterwards was probably the greatest thing in the life of young villagers . . . with its bell-ringing, organ, and choir, and outside activities . . . quite a glorious presence. Its morning service was full of dignity, its evensong of cheerfulness. The boys of the Grammar School attended in neat short jackets and faultless white collars; even the doctor never missed unless something really frightful kept him away. Apart from solemn and splendid occasions, the church at evening used to fill up in a remarkable way. You supposed that old So-and-So would never come into such a place; but there, as the single bell was ringing 'hurry', there he came, to sit in a side aisle with the rest. Excitement grew as the pews filled, and similarly in the vestry there was eager speculation over the strength of the choir that night. We could muster forty and more, though some might be rather social than musical contributors. The little boys saw with exclamations one and another old-timer come in, and hunt for a cassock and surplice, till with all the host assembled the vicar appeared with beaming countenance and a little joke, then the prayer; thereupon the choir marched up the aisle with lusty tune and all was happy.

Edmund attended the Grammar School and was then moved on to the 'great school in Sussex', namely Christ's Hospital. From there he won the Senior Classics scholarship to Queen's College, Oxford, in 1914, the year war was declared.

In 1915 he joined up; in the spring of 1916 was drafted with 11th Royal Sussex Regiment to serve in France; won the Military Cross; was gassed, but somehow survived two years of combat: front-line trench warfare of the most terrible kind.

> . . . At the noon of the dreadful day
> Our trench and death's is on a sudden stormed
> With huge and shattering salvoes, the clay dances
> In founts of clods around the concrete sties
> Where still the brain devises some last armour
> To live out the poor limbs.
>
> This wrath's oncoming
> Found four of us together in a pillbox,
> Skirting the abyss of madness with light phrases,
> White and blinking, in false smiles grimacing.
> The demon grins to see the game, a moment
> Passes, and – still the drum-tap dongs my brain
> To a whirring void – through the great breach above me
> The light comes in with icy shock and the rain
> Horridly drips. Doctor, talk, talk! if dead
> Or stunned I know not; the stinking powdered concrete,
> The lyddite turns me sick – my hair's all full
> Of this smashed concrete. O I'll drag you, friends,
> Out of the sepulchre into the light of day:
> For this is day, the pure and sacred day.
> And while I squeak and gibber over you,
> Out of the wreck a score of field-mice nimble,
> And tame and curious look about them. (These
> Calmed me, on these depended my salvation.)
>
> There comes my serjeant, and by all the powers
> The wire is holding to the right battalion
> And I can speak – but I myself first spoken
> Hear a known voice now measured even to madness
> Call me by name: 'for God's sake send and help us,
> Here in a gunpit, all headquarters done for,

Forty or more, the nine-inch came right through.
All splashed with arms and legs, and I myself
The only one not killed, not even wounded.
You'll send – God bless you.' The more monstrous fate
Shadows our own, the mind droops doubly burdened,
Nay all for miles our anguish groans and bleeds,
A whole sweet countryside amuck with murder,
Each moment puffed into a year with death.

Still wept the rain, roared guns,
Still swooped into the swamps of flesh and blood
All to the drabness of uncreation sunk,
And all thought dwindled to a moan, – Relieve!
But who with what command can now relieve
The dead men from that chaos, or my soul?

from 'Third Ypres – A Reminiscence'

Edmund emerged from war in November 1918, little more than twenty-two years old, but 'armistice brought no respite to his mind, and for the rest of his long life this "harmless young shepherd in a soldier's coat", as he described himself in "Undertones of War", continually thought, wrote, and dreamed of the horror of the trenches.' (Sir Rupert Hart-Davis on Edmund Blunden).

In 1920, Edmund went to live on Boar's Hill, near Oxford, home of other poets, among them Robert Graves. Around this time, he wrote a poem called 'An Ancient Goddess: In Two Pictures', in which he comes face to 'tombless face' with Graves's Goddess Muse, the Moon Goddess we met earlier (page 103). I say Graves's Goddess, but the beautiful, terrible vision, captivating but frightening, awesome in every way, is the imprisoner and liberator of *every* Muse poet: 'I cannot think of any true poet from Homer onwards,' Graves wrote, 'who has not independently recorded his experience of her.'

Edmund's Goddess, Phoebe too, 'impels the life we know' (namely poetry); she dotes upon the natural world; she is 'the enchantress of the skies' to whom all – even the tiniest flowers – sing. But she has this other side, her other 'Picture', which 'lures out the voiceless bird, unwarms the empty nest', and is a 'brooding badness in the air' –

What tragic Need impels *this* ghost into our sky?

The contradiction, which seemed to trouble Edmund all his adult life, is that, as Wordsworth put it, both pictures could be 'workings of one mind, the features of the same face' – a countenance writ both with the joy of childhood and the hell of war. In his poem, 'Report on Experience', he sums up his faith, an empirical resolution of the conflict. The contradiction is the human condition, but there is hope:

Over there are faith, life, virtue in the sun.

Report on Experience

I have been young, and now am not too old;
And I have seen the righteous forsaken,
His health, his honour and his quality taken.
    This is not what we were formerly told.

I have seen a green country, useful to the race,
Knocked silly with guns and mines, its villages vanished,
Even the last rat and the last kestrel banished –
    God bless us all, this was peculiar grace.

I knew Seraphina; Nature gave her hue,
Glance, sympathy, note, like one from Eden.
I saw her smile warp, heard her lyric deaden;
    She turned to harlotry; – this I took to be new.

Say what you will, our God sees how they run.
These disillusions are His curious proving
That He loves humanity and will go on loving;
    Over there are faith, life, virtue in the sun.

The church, seen from the swampy hollow of the Sands.

John Clare

b.1793

'I see him there, with his streaming hair . . .
Lit with a burning deathless discontent.'
Edmund Blunden in 'Clare's Ghost'

The story of John Clare's life is the stuff of romantic tragedy.

He was born in the village of Helpston, near Northampton, in the days before Enclosure of the common land. His father, Parker Clare, was a labourer and occasional wrestler. Post-harvest, as flail thresher, Parker would exercise his mighty arms across the road from the cottage where he lived with his wife, Ann, at Savage's barn. 'Savage' was the name of the farmer who owned the dark, stuffy barn, but an apt description too of the primitive nature of Parker's unenviable work.

> The thresher, dull as winter's day,
> And lost to all that spring displays,
> Still mid his barn-dust forced to stand,
> Swings round his flail with weary hand;
> While o'er his head shades thickly creep,
> That hides the blinking owl asleep
> And bats, in cobweb-corners bred,
> Sharing till night their bed,
> The sunshine trickles on the floor,
> Through every crevice of the door,
> This makes his barn, where shadows dwell,
> As irksome as a prisoner's cell.

Home – the cottage where John was born, he described as 'roomy and comfortable', and indeed it must have been, for one family. There is some contention in the village as to whether the Clares ever lived in all of the building that stands today, but we know that during their time there a change of landlord saw the house divided into four parts, John and his parents relieved of whatever roominess they had enjoyed, and confined to 'a corner of one room on a floor for three guineas a year and a little slip of the garden'.

Parker, being the sitting tenant of the cottage, got first choice in the garden carve-up and wisely retained the patch where a favoured apple tree, a Golden Russet, grew. 'Tho the ground was good for nothing yet the tree still befriended us,' John recalled later, '& made shift to make up the greater part of our rent.'

As a young boy, he had sparse formal education and both his

The cottage at Helpston, near Northampton, where John Clare was born.

'The thresher, dull as winter's day'.

mother and father were illiterate. He spent all the time he could on the common land around Helpston, making friends 'with the shepherds and herdboys as fancys prompted sometimes playing at marbles on the smooth-beaten sheeptracks or leapfrog among the thymy molehills', or picking red and blue flowers to stick in his cap and playing at soldiers, 'or running into the woods to hunt strawberries or stealing peas in churchtime when the owners were safe to boil at the gypseys fire.'

As time went on, he began to enjoy more solitary outings – 'I lovd this solitary disposition from a boy & felt a curiosity to wander about spots where I had never been before'. On one occasion, while on an errand to gather sticks from the wood, he succumbed to a long-felt temptation to explore the heathland just outside Helpston, then called 'Emmonsales stretching its yellow furze from my eye into unknown solitudes . . . I had imagind that the world's end was at the orizon & that a days journey was able to find it so I went . . . expecting when I got to the brink of the world that I coud look down like looking into a large pit & see into its secrets the same as I believd I coud see heaven by looking into the water'.

John walked and walked all day until 'the very wild flowers seemd to forget me . . . I imagind they were the inhabitants of new countrys'. He felt no fear – 'my wonder-seeking happiness had no room for it'. Eventually 'night came on' but before he had time to worry about that, 'the morning was by', and he decided to seek his home. He had no idea where he was or which direction to go, but by chance chose the right route – 'when I got home I found my

'Emmonsales stretching its yellow furze from my eye into unknown solitudes.'

parents in the great distress & half the village about hunting me'.

Clare wrote of what, as a boy, he observed in nature in prose as unfettered by grammatical dogma as his wanderings remained thankfully unrestrained by parental discipline:

I felt the most happy to be alone – with such merry company I heard the black and brown beetle sing their evening song with rapture & lovd to see the black snail steal out upon the dewy baulks
I saw the nimble horse bee at noon spinning on wanton wing I lovd to meet the woodman whistling away to his toils & to see the shepherd bending over his hook on the thistly greens chattering love storys to the listening milkmaid while she milkd her brindld cow

The first primrose in spring was as delightful as if seen for the first time & how the copper colord clouds of the morning was watchd

On Sundays I usd to feel a pleasure to hide in the woods instead of going to Church to nestle among the leaves & lye upon a mossy bank where the fir-like fern its under forest keeps . . .

I markd the varied colors in flat spreading fields checkered with closes of different tinted grain like the colors in a map the copper tinted colors of clover in blossom the sun-tanned green of the ripening hay the lighter hues of wheat and barley intermixd with the sunny glare of the yellow carlock & the sunset imitation of the scarlet headaches with the blue cornbottles crowding their splendid colors in large sheets over the land & troubling the cornfields with destroying beauty the different green of the woodland trees the dark oak the paler ash the mellow lime the white poplar peeping above the rest like leafy steeples the grey willow shining chilly in the sun as if the morning mist still lingered on its cool green I felt the beauty of these with eager delight the gadflys noonday hum the fainter murmur of the beefly

'spinning in the evening ray' the dragonflys in spangled coats darting like winged arrows down the thin stream the swallow darting through its one archd brig the shepherd hiding from the thunder shower in a hollow dotterel the wild geese skudding along & making all the letters of the alphabet as they flew the motley clouds the whispering wind that muttered to the leaves & summer grasses as it flitted among them like things at play
I observd all this with the same raptures as I have done since but I knew nothing of poetry. . .

Not all John's time was spent alone in the fields. He remembers Valentines Day – 'though young we were not without loves we had our favourites in the village & we listend the expected noises of creeping feet & the tinkling latch as eagerly as upgrown loves'.

For one girl in particular, he seems to have developed strong feelings: 'I was a lover very early in life my first attachment being a schoolboy affection'. Mary Joyce was the object of what John described as a 'romantic or Platonic sort of feeling', a girl 'who cost me more ballads than sighs. . .

if I coud but gaze on her face or fancy a smile on her countenance it was sufficient . . . we played with each other but named nothing of love yet I fancyd her eyes told me her affections we walked together as school-companions in leisure hours but our talk was of play & our actions the wanton nonsense of children yet young as my heart was it woud turn chill when I touchd her hand & tremble & I fancyd her feelings were the same for as I gazd earnestly in her face a tear would hang in her smiling eye & she woud turn to wipe it away her heart was as tender as a birds. . .

Like Richard Jefferies, John's education in the fields did not prepare him for manhood, nor was he suited physically to a labourer's occupation or temperamentally, it seems, to any.

In preparation, respectively, for work as shoemaker and stone-mason, John was taught 'cross-multiplication for the one & bills of account for the other but I was not to be either'.

When his parents began to doubt his excuses not to work, 'I whimperd & turnd a sullen eye upon every occasion till they gave me my will . . . they thought I had been born with a dislike to work & a view to have my liberty and remain idle . . . they woud not urge me to anything against my will so I livd on at home taking work as it fell'.

He was employed 'weeding wheat in the spring with old women listening to their songs & stories'; in summer he joined the haymakers in the fields. When the seasons no longer offered him work he'd gather sticks in the wood or pick up 'dried cow-dung in the pasture which we call cazons for firing'. And all the time he longed to resume the freedom and joys of childhood. Guiltily he'd steal away to play once more with 'shepherders or herdboys in

Helpston church: 'by yon spire that points to heaven/Where my earliest vows was given.' When they grew up, Mary Joyce rejected him, and in John's mind became the mesmeric focus of all that was beautiful in his childhood, and ultimately unattainable.

'I love to walk the fields they are to me
A legacy no evil can destroy'.

lone spots out of sight for I had grown big enough to be ashamed of it & I felt a sort of hopeless prospect around me of not being able to meet manhood'.

Again like Richard Jefferies, matters were made worse by his always having 'that feeling of ambition about me that wishes to gain notice or to rise above my fellows'.

It was around this time that John first had the Dream.

The first dream in which she appeared to me was when I had not written a line . . . she suddenly came to my old house led me out in a hurried manner – into the field called Maple hill & there placed me on the top where I could see an immense crowd all around me in the north west quarter of the field towards Hilly wood and Swordy.

[Soldiers appeared on horseback] moving in evolutions of exercise & the rest were crowds of various description on foot as at a great fair where ladies in splendid dresses were most numerous but the finest lady in my own heart's opinion was the lady at my side – I felt shamed into insignificance at the sight & seemed to ask her from my own thoughts why I had been so suddenly brought into such immense company when my only life & care was being alone & to myself –

you are the only one of the crowd now she said & hurried me back

& the scene turned to a city where she led me to what appeared to be a booksellers shop where I reluctantly followed

she said something to the owner of the place who stood behind a counter when he smiled

& at his back on a shelf among a vast crowd of books were three vols lettered with my own name – I see them now . . .

turning to look in her face I was awake in a moment.

John Clare calls her his 'Guardian spirit', 'a soul stirring beauty', who in later dreams 'moved my ideas into exstacy', she was his 'good genius & I believe in her ideally almost as fresh as reality'. She was 'a woman deity' who 'gave the sublimest consceptions of beauty to my imagination'.

In another dream, when 'the sun seemed of a pale moonstruck light – the sky had a dull unnatural hue', she accompanies him to Helpston church –

she was in white garments beautifully disordered but sorrowful in her countenance yet I instantly knew her face again – when we got into the church a light streamed in one corner of the chancel & from that light appeared to come the final decision of man's actions in life

I felt awfully afraid tho not terrified & in a moment my name was called from the north east corner of the chancel when my conductress smiled in exstacy & uttered something as prophetic of happiness

I knew all was right & she led me again into the open air when I imperceivably awoke to the sound of soft music – I felt delighted and sorrowful & talked to her awake for a moment as if she was still bending over me

The feeling of awe does not subside with the dream, it takes him over completely, revolutionises his life. Within a few years this hopeless, apparently indolent day labourer is a literary celebrity consorting with the likes of Lamb, Hazlitt and Coleridge at the home of his London publisher.

'Poems Descriptive of Rural Life and Scenery' appeared in 1820 and was followed by three other volumes published during the next fifteen years.

For subject matter, he turned – (he could not have looked elsewhere) – to the landscape of his childhood, finding in the Great Change wrought upon the land and the common man by the Enclosure system an exact and illuminating parallel with the fruitless taming of childhood freedoms, the enslavement of nature's child by man.

Enclosure of the open fields, of the common land, was the most radical event in the history of the English landscape. In the fire of the passion it instilled in him, he kindled his longing for the bliss of youth.

The common land had been wild, open, bleak, full of trees, birds, weeds, brambles, ants and snail-shells – it was the land that God intended, akin to the Garden of Eden. Now the woodman had moved in, his 'cruel axe employ'd A tree beheaded, or a bush destroy'd . . . all old favourites, fond taste approves, Griev'd me at heart to witness their removes.'

Ah what a paradise begins with life & what a wilderness the knowledge of the world discloses Surely the Garden of Eden was nothing more than our first parents entrance upon life & the loss of it their knowledge of the world.

In 'Childhood Recollections' Clare recalls the land of his childhood prior to the spoiling:

> Here winds the dyke where oft we jump'd across,
>   'Tis just as if it were but yesternight;
> There hangs the gate we call'd our wooden horse,
>   Where we in swee-swaw riding took delight.
>
> And everything shines round me just as then,
>   Mole-hills, and trees, and bushes speckling wild,

'There hangs the gate we call'd our wooden horse,/Where we in swee-swaw riding took delight.'

> That freshen all those pastimes up agen –
> Oh, grievous day that chang'd me from a child!

But in 'Remembrances' the physical consequences to the countryside of Enclosure make plain the scale of change and the nature of
Clare's 'lost content' –

> Enclosure like a Buonaparte let not a thing remain,
> It levelled every bush and tree and levelled every hill
> And hung the moles for traitors – though the brook is running still . . .

Trees, bushes, even meadows lost to the axe or 'never-weary
plough', leave 'a desert strange and chill', where even the moles
are killed and hung in chains – the wild landscape of youth is gone:

> . . . I see the little mouldiwarps hang sweeing to the wind
> On the only aged willow that in all the field remains,
> And nature hides her face while they're sweeing in their chains
> And in a silent murmuring complains . . .

> Oh, I never thought that joys would run away from boys,
> Or that boys would change their minds and forsake such summer joys . . .

What is real is gone, an image in the mind. Like Herbert Read,
Clare begins to see his life as an echo – 'the only real experiences
in life being those lived with a virgin sensibility. . . All life is an
echo of our first sensations'.

> The spring of our life – our youth – is the midsummer of our happiness – our
> pleasures are then real and heart stirring – they are but associations
> afterwards – where we laughed in childhood at the reality of the enjoyment
> felt we only smile in manhood at the recollections of these enjoyments they
> are then but the reflections of past happiness & have no more to do with
> happiness in reality than the image of a beautiful girl seen in a looking-glass
> has in comparison with the original –
> our minds only retain the resemblance
> the glass is as blank after her departure
> – we only feel the joy we possessed

With no real joy left to describe, the poet's work becomes more
lyrical than descriptive. He hypnotises himself with the melancholy of childhood loss, even identifying his Goddess Muse with the
unreal, idealised, unattainable childhood sweetheart, Mary Joyce
– his 'simple Enchantress', 'my witching love', 'the muse of every
song I write'.

Clare had begun his fatal drift away from reality and his Goddess
rejected him, mercilessly.

The idiosyncratic nature of his work – dialect, phonetic spellings, his unease with punctuation ('that awkward squad of pointings,' as he called it) are, in their own unique way, evocative of sense but they are also symbols of his work's downright truth. 'Honest Jack', 'Random Jack' were the names he liked to call himself. Believe it or not, he received criticism from some quarters for the lack of intellectual calculation in his work. Clare's best work was pure description inspired by melancholic joy. He was a pure medium for the Muse of his dreams and became her slave. It was a condition that inspired the theme of his poetry – enslavement of the honest labourer by the exploitive landowner, enslavement of wild nature by Enclosure, enslavement of nature's child by man – but finally broke him.

The later, lyrical style of this overnight star in the literary firmament, seeming almost mannered in comparison, was less successful. His Goddess – along with a fickle public for whom 'ploughman poets' were suddenly no longer in vogue – deserted him, and John Clare's descent into insanity was swift.

In his poem, 'The Nightmare', he describes it happening. Clare discovers the Goddess's other, cruel side, as she lets him go, and, like Edmund Blunden, sniffs that 'brooding badness in the air':

> She seemed at first as living beauty seems,
> Then changed more lovely in the shade of dreams;
> Then faded dim, confused, and hurrying by
> Like memory waning into vacancy . . .

> Something drew near me and my guide withdrew,
> Beauteous as ever but in terror too;
> Her bright eyes lessened dim but not with tears,
> Heavy with sorrows and the gloom of fears;
> And scarce I turned her desert flight to trace
> Ere a foul fiend seemed standing in her place.
> 'Twas Mary's voice that hung in her farewell. . .

> The fiend drew near to make my terrors ache –
> Huge circles lost to eyes, and rotten hulls
> Raised with dread groans from the dread 'place of skulls', –
> Then turned with horrid laugh its haggard head
> To where the earth-loved shadow dimly fled,
> As mockery – waking hell with horrid sound
> Like many murmurs moving underground.

In 1837 he was admitted to the insane asylum at High Beach, Epping. Four years later, with the help of a gipsy who pointed out the route, he escaped and walked for days with one thing in mind, to find Mary and his lost childhood. His recollections of the

'July 18 1841 Felt very melancholly went a walk in the forest in the afternoon – fell in with some gipseys one of whom offered to assist in my escape from the madhouse by hiding me in his camp . . . On Sunday I went & they were all gone.'

journey from Essex to Northamptonshire, particularly the indignities he suffered, make specially sad and painful reading because they are delivered to us in seeming sanity; he is finally reduced to satisfying his hunger 'by eating the grass by the road side which seemed to taste something like bread I was hungry & eat heartily till I was satisfied & in fact the meal seemed to do me good'. Eventually 'a cart passed me with a man & a woman & a boy in it when nearing me the woman jumped out & caught fast hold of my hands & wished me to get into the cart but I refused & thought her either drunk or mad'. It turns out that the woman is his wife. They arrive home, 'but Mary was not there neither could I get any information about her further than the old story of her being dead six years ago . . . but I took no notice of the blarney having seen her myself about a twelvemonth ago alive & well & as young as ever.'

Henry Williamson

b. 1895

'Lacking the father-hero vision on which to grow spiritually sound, he made his own wilderness vision . . . through poetic feeling.' The Dark Lantern

The Great War changed Henry Williamson's life. The muddy, bloody, horror of trench warfare, described so powerfully in 'The Patriot's Progress', had nothing to do with it, though he emerged from it in a state of nervous exhaustion.

What, in the Great War, changed Williamson's life was the mercy and kindness, the fraternity of war, something he professed to have found little of at home.

He enlisted in the 1st Battalion of the London Rifle Brigade in the summer of 1914 and sailed for France on November 4th, little more than three weeks short of his nineteenth birthday.

One night when he was walking away from the trenches a comrade was hit in the ankle and fell upon the barbed wire in No Man's Land where he lay, hanging, unable to move. Williamson went to his aid, shouting, 'I'm coming to the rescue of my comrade.' The firing ceased, an officer of the German army helped him remove the wounded man, saluted, and turned away.

On Christmas Day, that same year, as Williamson was walking back from the front-line dug-out that he had occupied during an attack, he happened to turn back and noticed, as he looked towards No Man's Land, that there had been struck, spontaneously, between the two front lines, a truce. During an extraordinary day of harmony between the opposing sides, he fell into conversation with a young soldier of the 133rd Saxon Regiment in front of the Bois de Ploegsteer. Though he didn't realise it until later, the experience altered his entire conception of the world.

The surprise fraternization, coming spontaneously out of the most appalling disunity, slaughter and mayhem, seems to have given Williamson a glimpse of a higher, spiritual majesty.

What particularly struck him was not only the spiritual harmony, but its occurrence out of utter disunity.

Williamson took his war-time experiences as a sign of the coming of a New Age of spiritual energy – the 'age of sun, of harmony', as he referred to it, and there was a strong sense that the Age had been released upon the human race out of exhilarating awesome incident, the orchestrated hell of his first wartime offensive, which he described as 'magnificent . . . like the end of Wagner's "The Ring".'

After Armistice, when Williamson first picked up a copy of 'The Story of My Heart', its author, the 'primitive', Richard Jefferies (see page 111), became his idol. He wrote of him: 'He was a genius, a visionary whose thought and feeling were wide as the human world, prophet of an age not yet come into being. . .'

Henry Williamson took to Jefferies because he recognised himself – his own nature – in him. He recognised a kindred spirit. He didn't become like Jefferies, as has been suggested; he was already like him, and fancied he had suffered as a boy like him. Coming out of the War, nerves jangling, Williamson stood awestruck as Jefferies revealed to him through his spiritual autobiography (and with perfect timing), that he had shared in a spiritual enlightenment similar to Williamson's at the Front.

In Williamson's foreword to his own quartet of novels 'The Flax of Dreams', published in 1936, he summarises what he sees as the portent of his and Jefferies' spiritual experience by quoting a long passage from 'The Incalculable Hour' by J Quiddington West, which suggests that 'we are turning again to the ancient founts of wisdom, the ancient forgotten beauty that our fathers knew and loved with a passionate love. To the watchful eyes, signs are not wanting that a new spiritual world is coming to birth – that we are on the eve of a great spiritual change.'

Unfortunately for him (because people failed to understand where Williamson's argument was coming from, and they turned on him), in the same foreword he hailed Adolf Hitler as champion of this spiritual rebirth.

Williamson had been to Germany, witnessed the rallies, been carried away by the mass emotion, 'when millions of men and women had cheered their leader and national inspirer . . . The feeling I had while among the masses of people listening to Adolf Hitler at Nuremberg was one of their happiness and goodness.' He might have said that he had received a sense of Wagnerian glory.

And so, in the 'Flax of Dreams' foreword he wrote, 'I salute the great man across the Rhine, whose life symbol is the happy child', and when war was inevitable he was promptly interned.

The truth that Williamson seems to have grasped is that without disunity there can be no harmony; without chaos there can be no serenity – 'serenity through love' was Williamson's dearest wish; without ugliness there can be no beauty; without hate there can be no love. It is a condition of nature – life on earth – that not one of these could be defined or recognised were it not for the fact that its opposite also exists. He saw that the special spirit of fraternity revealed to him in 1914 would not have occurred if it had not been for the horror of war.

He was not justifying war. His was a Big Bang theory of

spiritual rejuvenation, centred, mythically, on the sun. It is unlikely, however, that he felt that the human race needed a second war in which its spiritual salvation might be brewed. He accorded Hitler the role of prophet because he had observed him at close quarters in the pre-War years in Germany; he saw a man who, like him, had served in the ranks in the First War, had been wounded and blinded with mustard gas, a man who must, surely, have shared the same spiritual enlightenment as himself.

Williamson was swept up in the emotional hysteria of the time.

And to be fair to him, it was a hysteria that history would show was sufficiently strong to prepare a whole people to close its eyes and blindly follow a lunatic leader.

Here, so it seemed to Williamson in 1936, was the great swell of emotion needed for the Big Change, the Age of Sun, and it was not incidental that he included in his salute that telling phrase, 'whose symbol is the happy child'. For everything that Williamson was, and so much of his work, even the interpretation he laid upon that extraordinary Christmas Day back in 1914, was – as everything is for all of us – rooted in his own childhood.

Williamson was born near London at Brockley, where, in those days, the countryside met the city. He was the son of a bank clerk.

In 'The Dark Lantern', the first volume of his 15-book 'A Chronicle of Ancient Sunlight', we meet what is almost certainly Williamson's own family: the unimaginative, lower middle-class, unfulfilled Richard Maddison and his wife, Hettie, a loving mother but a wife always too eager to please.

It seems that there was opposition set up almost immediately between father and a son who grew up to detest the suburban veil of gentility, respectability, and values grounded in fear, behind which they lived. His father's ambitions had come to naught and he had retreated, subjecting the family to an unhappy vision of life as tedious duty.

Repressing his natural paternal feelings along with any other true signal of warmth, the father crippled the son's natural filial affection. They lived in an emotional No Man's Land without even festive pause for fraternization, a minefield which, when son became 'as aggrieved in spirit as was the father', erupted in explosive retort. What eventually resolved *this* chaos was a love and understanding of nature that fulfilled the artist in the man.

Like Richard Jefferies before him, as a boy Henry found freedom from familial discord, in nature. He depended for his salvation upon family holidays in Norfolk and the West Country, and every Wednesday and Saturday, as his biographer Daniel Farson tells us, the schoolboy would cycle off to Holme Park woods in Kent where his interest was in the birds and animals and the freedom of life there. The woods were young Henry's fantasy land, – 'A child lacking love forms itself alone. It will live mainly in a world of fantasy,' he once wrote.

In his first book, 'The Beautiful Years', the first of four novels that make up 'The Flax of Dreams', which, if not declared autobiography, Williamson allowed is 'autopsychical', he relives an experience he had had when about twelve in Holme Park woods.

They are forbidden territory. When, later, the trespassing of Willie and Rupert is discovered, Willie, the boy hero, is thrashed by his father.

They were in the forbidden forest.

A magpie chattered before they had gone fifty yards, and they crouched in silence. A blackbird shrilled, and a wren commenced its 'tick-tack' warning.

'It's not a keeper,' whispered Willie, 'for wrens don't call out for a man. I expect we've disturbed an old owl. Come on, man, it's quite safe. Aren't the bluebells ripping?'

They then went on, then paused to listen. Somewhere a nightingale was singing; around them warblers and whitethroats were uttering husky, jarring threads of song, all in ecstasy; winding in and out of the hazel wands, their vanes splashed with gold as they passed through a rift in the leaves where the sunlight came, humming gently, went the wild humble-bees, called from buttercup and heavy-odoured nettle by the chimes of scent pealed from the bluebells. With joy Willie noticed that Rupert was entranced, for he had brought him here, *he* was showing him the beauties that so few boys seemed to love . . . a rabbit rushed away among the brambles, almost from under their feet; their hearts thumped as with tremendous whir of wings and hoarse, quick crowing a cock pheasant rose and flew away.

'I say,' whispered Rupert, smiling feebly.

Willie whispered that it was all right – somehow it was natural to whisper among the greeneries of the wood.

Warily the two boys crept along a path, beaten and imprinted with hobnailed boots, all leading the same way.

At any moment Willie knew that they might have to run for their lives. Oh, there was romance and adventure!

Round a bend in the pathway they came upon a small hut, with the door open. Peering in the cobwebbed window, they saw an old coat hanging on a nail, a besom broom, several pheasant cages – made of wood to trap hen birds – rusted and terrible gins, bottles, spades, and other things. Round the other side of the hut was a tall oak, and upon its bole were nailed things that made them gaze in silence. There were many dead creatures, hedge-pigs and cats among them, tier upon tier of them. Magpies and jays alternated with the brown kestrel hawks and crows. There were dozens of hawks, scores of weasels and stoats, all in various stages of decay and desolation. Of some only the head remained, others had been shot or trapped that morning. But the most pathetic of all were the owls.

'Round the other side of the hut was a tall oak, and upon its bole were nailed things that made him gaze in silence. . .

'What is it?' Rupert whispered.

'A vermin pole. . . '

A scream came from somewhere near, and they clutched each other.

'What is it Willie?' Rupert whispered.

'I don't know.'

'Let's explore.'

'Go carefully.'

Quietly they went towards the sound, but could find nothing.

Another scream, not so loud but hoarser, caused them to look to one side.

Upon a big piece of turf, supported three feet from the ground by four sticks, stood a jay. They went nearer, and saw that it was caught in a trap, that the jagged teeth had sprung together and broken the thighs. Its mouth was open, as though to breathe more air, its crest raised in pain. Its poor eyes looked at them wistfully, its poor breast fluttered. Blood had clotted the thin frailty of its legs; the bones were smashed.

'Oh, oh,' sobbed Rupert.

'It's trapped,' said Willie, 'look, the keeper has put some rotten pheasants' eggs to tempt it, and hidden that gin underneath . . .

They took the broken thing from the iron trap and killed it.

'It's against the law,' cried Willie fiercely, 'jays are protected. I looked on the police board. It's all wrong.'

'Shall we tell a copper?'

'A copper?' sneered Willie, 'aren't we trespassing?'

The other looked frightened.

'I will tell you what I'm going to do,' he went on. 'I'm going to tear up every damhell trap in this wood, that's what I'm going to do! And what's more no one shall stop me. No one! Do you hear?'

After half an hour they had destroyed eleven. William grew careless in his righteous lust for destruction. 'Ha! one more, Rupey,' – common idealism had apparently welded still more firmly their friendship – 'that makes twelve. Now then, we'll rip this up – Oh, Billo man! Run, quick!' he shrilled in terror, for an under-keeper had crept to within fifty yards of them.

In terror the two pathetic knights spurred their crowlegged steeds and fled before the keeper. Their mouths dried with the thought of capture; imagination sapped their strength. Willie took Rupert's hand and pulled him along, but steadily the thudding footfalls of their pursuer drew nearer. He shouted as he ran. 'Fred! Fred!' and at each bellow their hearts thumped sickeningly. Rupert's feet moved slower and slower; his eyes protruded from his head in agony.

'I'm done, man,' he sobbed.

'Come on,' wailed Willie, 'he's dead beat himself.'

'Fred! Fred!' bellowed the keeper.

Someone shouted in front.

What use was further endeavour?

They collapsed on the ground, gasping, with red faces and matted hair. Willie was immediately sick.

Fred came up, and pounced upon them. He had once been a groom, and came from Wapping.

'I knows 'un,' he growled, 'lives in Rookhurst. I knows 'un.'

'I knows 'un,' he growled, 'lives in Rookhurst. I knows 'un.'

Unlike Richard Jefferies, whose compassion led him late in life to see the hunter instinct in nature as 'anti-human', Williamson's attitude to nature became one of unquestioning understanding. He accepted the hunter mentality of man and animal, even on one occasion calling upon his own experience in war to elucidate the sensations of the hunted stag and draw the myth of cruelty of the hunt. At the same time he loved animals, and some humans, for their spirit. He was fascinated by life, all life. Once Williamson admitted 'a secret solitary feeling which I hardly dared expose even to myself in my thoughts' while watching a weasel circling a rat and identifying with the rat's 'helpless desire, sharp-sweet, deadly cloying, to give itself to the hunter'.

This is the empathic apogee of the true naturalist who sees nature as it is, not as he, or someone else, might like it to be. It is the reality, the background from which Williamson's sense of beauty emerged and derived its bite.

Returning from the War, Williamson antagonised his father with thoughts of living by writing, an idea his father dismissed as an excuse for idleness. The dutiful bank clerk, up every morning to go to work on time, became furious with a son who laid in bed and spoke absurdly, dramatically, arrogantly, about his spiritual vision of the world that would be the subject of his writing.

Soon, when his de-mob money ran out, Henry had to get a job anyway, and ground his idealism on the rough surface of the

Classified Advertising Department of the Times, selling space during the day, and feeding his spirit at night in his bedroom, writing 'The Beautiful Years', with a tame owl perched on the back of his chair.

But the bitterness between son and father at home could not continue. Eventually, we are told, all came to a head when Henry's extolling the virtues of the German soldier proved too much for his father, who named him 'Traitor!' and, despite his wife's last-minute pleas for leniency, threw him out of the house into the dead of night.

Henry left London and drove on his motorbike to Georgeham in North Devon, where he had spent many a happy holiday.

What a relief it must have been all round.

In Georgeham, at last, Henry could put to the test his childhood fantasy, and begin the quest for his own brand of content, for that 'ancient, forgotten beauty that our fathers knew and loved with a passionate love', which some men call truth.

He found it when he stopped writing about himself.

In a strange sort of way, otters linked every aspect of Henry's growth. He saw his first one on holiday in Norfolk as a teenager; the next in a disused German gun emplacement during the War, and the third was introduced to him at Skirr Cottage which he rented in Georgeham. He helped a friend rescue the model for

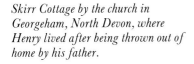

Skirr Cottage by the church in Georgeham, North Devon, where Henry lived after being thrown out of home by his father.

To the menagerie of animals that roamed wild at Skirr Cottage was added an otter cub which Henry had helped rescue from a drain. He gave it to his cat, who had her own kitten, to nurse.

The Torridge valley – Tarka country:
'Time flowed with the sunlight of the

Tarka from a drain running down to a river, and later had his cat rear it as part of her litter. It became part of his life, an integral part of a whole menagerie of 'dogs, cats, gulls, buzzards, magpies' that Eleanor Graham tells us lived in Skirr cottage on more or less equal terms with Henry.

Then one night it strayed and Henry, with the help of his dog, Billjohn, found it caught in a gin-trap. He threw his jacket over the chattering animal and managed to release the trap, but the otter ran off, apparently having lost three of its toes in the trap's jaws. For hours Henry searched, but failed to find him.

One stormy night a year or two later he fancied he saw him in the churchyard next to Skirr Cottage, when two eyes glinted up at him in the moonlight, but he couldn't be sure.

At the end of 'Tarka' – the terrible hunt itself – after six hours of wearying chase, there is a pause, a stillness, a peace, a serenity: a moment in time made poignant by the expectation of more carnage to come.

It's as if Williamson is holding up a cross-section of his vision of life-on-earth. The closer we look at it, the more microscopically observant the writer becomes, the more exquisitely truthful seems the picture – even the beautiful, dainty, fairy-winged dragonfly is a hunter, 'seizing flies and tearing them apart in its horny jaws'. In 'Tarka' Williamson is not decrying the hunting of wild animals. This *is* nature. We should not be deceived. This is what's on offer, life on earth – both the darkness and the light. Wonder at it in all its glory.

still green place . . . the otters hunted and ragrowstered for many days under

the high wooded hills below which the river wound and coiled like a serpent.'

Canal Bridge on the river Torridge, near Weare Giffard, where Henry Williamson planned his book and beneath which, in a riverside holt, Tarka was born.

Here, also, Tarka 'was seen no more' and, on the very day that the hunt scene was shot here for the film of Tarka, August 13th, 1977, his creator died.

But the little girl, who shares Tarka's secret, has the spirit of the place, and there is a sense in Williamson's writing of the 'splendour of purpose fulfilled'.

During the sixth hour the otter disappeared. The river grew quiet. People not in uniform sat down on the grass. The huntsman was wading slowly upstream, feeling foothold with pole and keeping an eye on Deadlock. Stickle stood slack, but ready to bar the way with pole-strokes. Look-outs gazed at the water before them. It was known that the otter might leave the river at any moment. The boy with the warped pole, on whose cheeks were two patches of dried otter-blood, was already opening his knife, ready to cut another notch on the handle in the form of a cross.

But for more than an hour the sun-thongs flickered across the placid water; and in softening light the owl returned, flying high over the bridge, to the mouse runs in the quiet meadow beyond.

A fallen bough of willow lay in the pool near one bank, and Tarka lay beside it. His rudder held a sunken branch. Only his wide upper nostrils were above the water. He never moved. Every yard of the banks between the stickles was searched again. Poles were thrust into branches, roots, and clumps of flag-lilies. The wading huntsman prodded Peal Rock and the rock

The weir, up-river from the Canal Bridge. 'The summer water tumbled down the fish-pass, but glided thin as a snail's shell over the top end of the concrete sill. The lower end by the fender at the head of the leat was dry.' Here, Tarka stretched out in the sun before being disturbed by Shiner, the poacher, and the hound, Pitiful, and escaping across country to Canal Bridge, for the last time.

A full walker's guidebook, 'The Tarka Trail', is part of a conservation initiative called the Tarka Project, based at Torrington, Devon EX38 8EZ.

above it. Hounds sat on the banks, shivering, and watching Deadlock, Render, and Harper working the banks. The crack of a whip, a harsh voice rating – Rufus had turned a rabbit out of a bramble and was chasing it across the meadow. He returned to the river in a wide circle, eyeing the whip.

At the beginning of the eighth hour a scarlet dragonfly whirred and darted over the willow snag, watched by a girl sitting on the bank. Her father, an old man lank and humped as a heron, was looking out near her. She watched the dragonfly settle on what looked like a piece of bark beside the snag; she heard a sneeze, and saw the otter's whiskers scratch the water. Glancing round she realised that she alone had seen the otter. She flushed, and hid her grey eyes with her lashes. Since childhood she had walked the Devon rivers with her father, looking for flowers and the nests of birds, passing some rocks and trees as old friends, seeing a Spirit everywhere, gentle in thought to all her eyes beheld.

For two minutes the maid sat silent, hardly daring to look at the river. The dragonfly flew over the pool, seizing flies and tearing them apart in its horny jaws. Her father watched it as it settled on the snag, rose up, circled, and lit on the water, it seemed. Tarka sneezed again, and the dragonfly flew away. A grunt of satisfaction from the old man, a brown hand and wrist holding aloft a hat, a slow intake breath, and,

'TALLY-HO!'

Beatrix Potter

b. 1866

'Thoughts of that peaceful past of childhood come like soft music and a blissful vision through the snow . . .'

Helen Beatrix Potter was born in 1866 at No. 2 Bolton Gardens, Kensington – her 'unloved birthplace' as she later described it. Her father, Rupert, a barrister, was not a success professionally; he had only one brief and that turned out to be a hoax. No matter, he had inherited wealth (from the cotton mills of the North) and instead pursued photography as a hobby, becoming technically highly proficient.

Rupert and his wife, Helen, led quiet, predictable lives – he would go to his club each day, while she in her well-mannered way would visit other ladies in the area at a fixed time every afternoon. Everything was well ordered, and everybody (especially Beatrix and the servants) knew their place. Strict routines quelled even the possibility of surprise – there were never any parties to vary it – and the drudgery infected the whole personality of the house, which an irreverent cousin once described as 'a dark Victorian mausoleum, complete with aspidistras'.

Here, Beatrix, a child alone until she was five when her brother Bertram was born, would 'watch things pass', measuring time by her parents' coming and going and the never-failing beat of a grandfather clock that echoed up the cold staircase to her third-floor chamber. It was a lonely sanitised confinement, for Beatrix rarely saw her parents other than in a formal drawing-room situation. Her nurse, McKenzie, a starchy Scot of Calvinist principles, would take her for a walk once a day, but otherwise Beatrix rarely went out. She didn't even go to school – 'I fancy I could have been taught anything if I had been caught young,' she once wrote, 'but it was in the days when parents kept governesses, and only boys went to school in most families.' As a result, and because she never went out to play, she had no friends at all, and became a shy wallflower of a little person. On the few occasions that she attended a party for her cousins she'd sit quite alone on a chair in a corner, and the Potters' coachman or maid knew to collect her in good time.

Once in a while – to her great delight – she would be dropped off at Camfield Place, a 300-acre estate in Hertfordshire which her grandfather had bought in the year of her birth. There she would find her way to her favourite place to sit – a cross-bar beneath a huge table in the library – clutching a beloved flanelette pig and listening to the voice of her grandmother the other side of the heavy drapes of the green-fringed tablecloth.

With a start such as this, who would want to grow up? Yet somehow, instead of turning in on herself and dying inside, Beatrix blossomed into an extraordinary talent. She did so partly because she was blessed with a quite unusual imagination which, though force-fed on solitariness at home, received precious nourishment on holidays to the country from the age of five. Partly, too, she survived because she met her childhood lot with an instinctual fortitude, a courage born (she claimed) out of an hereditary affinity with the 'native Cromptom rock' on which her Scottish grandmother was born, and which Beatrix believed had somehow filtered into her own personality.

The Potter holidays were an attempt by Rupert to get his social life going. Bolton Gardens may not have been conducive to the party spirit, but up in Perthshire, at Birnam, where he rented a holiday villa called Heath Park, and at the family's favourite retreat nearby – Dalguise – Rupert could offer country pursuits – shooting and fishing – to visitors, and as his photography of the period shows he was not unsuccessful in attracting some eminent people as guests.

Among them Beatrix found, to her astonishment, the first adults to offer her genuine friendship. There was Sir John Millais, the Pre-Raphaelite painter: 'I shall always have a most affectionate remembrance of Sir John Millais,' she wrote later, 'though unmercifully afraid of him as a child, on account of what the papers call "his schoolboy manner". I had a brilliant colour as a little girl, which he used to provoke on purpose and remark upon at times. If a great portrait painter's criticism is of any interest this is it, delivered with due consideration, turning me round under a window, that I was a little like his daughter Carrie, at that time a fine handsome girl, but my face was spoiled by the length of my nose and upper lip.'

Then there was Mr Gaskell, husband of the famous novelist, less of a tease but full of genuine and welcome affection; and the Quaker politician John Bright who came alive in her company, read her poems in his 'low-pitched, magnificent voice' and took her exploring, on one occasion 'discovering' a harp played long ago by Mary Queen of Scots in an old deserted dower house. These were adults who understood something of being a child. They warmed to the pretty, quiet little girl who seemed so self-contained and withdrawn. They were a revelation to Beatrix.

'Mr Gaskell is sitting comfortably in the warm sunshine on the doorstep at Dalguise, in his grey coat and old felt hat. The newspaper lies on his knees, suddenly he looks up with his gentle smile. There are sounds of pounding footsteps. The blue-bottles whizz off the path. A little girl in a print frock and striped stockings bounds to his side and offers him a bunch of meadowsweet. He just says, "Thank you, dear", and puts his arm round her.'

The bridge leading from the garden to the house at Dalguise. 'I remember every stone, every tree. . . Even when the thunder growled in the distance, and the wind swept up the valley in fitful gusts, oh, it was always beautiful.'

But it wasn't just people that raised her spirits, it was the sheer beauty of the countryside – 'It sometimes happens,' she wrote when she was seventy, 'that the town child is more alive to the fresh beauty of the country than a child who is country born . . .' Dalguise in particular made an indelible impression: 'I remember every stone, every tree, the scent of the heather, the music sweetest mortal ears can hear, the murmuring of the wind through the fir trees. Even when the thunder growled in the distance, and the wind swept up the valley in fitful gusts, oh, it was always beautiful.'

Empathy flowed between Beatrix and what she saw. The animal world – like her own, she perceived – was a 'pleasant unchanging world of realism and romance, which in our northern clime is stiffened by hard weather, a tough ancestry, and the strength that comes from the hills.' The animals and insects absorbed in their own private worlds were of necessity self-sufficient – just as she had learned to be in her lonely third-floor garret in Kensington. But here the animals had a fit context for going about their daily tasks; the naturalness of the scene lay in stark contrast to the artificial regime of London life. What was so real here was courted by Beatrix's imagination until, inevitably in one so steadfast and talented, it was expressed in her art. At Dalguise –

everything was romantic in my imagination. The woods were peopled by the mysterious good folk. The Lords and Ladies of the last century walked with me along the overgrown paths, and picked the old-fashioned flowers among the box and rose hedges of the garden. Half believing the picturesque superstitions of the district, seeing my own fancies so clearly that they became true to me, I lived in a separate world.

And then she began to draw.

I do not remember a time when I did not try to invent pictures and make for myself a fairyland amongst the wild flowers, the animals, fungi, mosses, woods and streams, all the thousand objects of the countryside.

John Millais stopped teasing her about her own beauty and began actively encouraging her.

He gave me the kindest encouragement with my drawings . . . he really paid me a compliment for he said that 'plenty of people can draw, but you and my son John have observation'.

She became something of a protégé of Millais, and though her early water colours were turned down by London galleries who could not take 'this shy slip of a girl' seriously, the friendship undoubtedly had a lasting effect on her style: 'When I was young,' she wrote many years later to a friend, 'it was still permissible to admire the Pre-Raphaelites; their somewhat niggling but absolute genuine fascination for copying natural details did certainly influence me.'

Her love of drawing, and the close observation and authenticity that characterised it, attracted another catalyst. Also on the estate at Dalguise she met Charles MacIntosh, a long-haired eccentric botanist, a specialist in fungi engaged in field research in the area, and quite a character besides, as Beatrix describes: 'Before his left fingers were cut off by a circular saw [he] was a real fiddler and even now by indomitable energy plays the 'cello. He seldom spoke but was sometimes heard to whistle. As to the weather he could never be induced to say more than 'Ahem'. I forget how many miles he used to walk. Some mathematical person reckoned it up. His successor had a tricycle. It will save his legs but modern habits and machines are not calculated to bring out individuality

Charles MacIntosh, the eccentric postman and botanist, became Beatrix's friend and advisor. 'He seldom spoke but was sometimes heard to whistle.'

or the study of natural history.' Immediately, MacIntosh and Beatrix had one thing in common, they were both very very shy. It's not clear who 'broke the ice', but Beatrix first spotted him in the woods searching for mushrooms – 'a more startled scarecrow would be difficult to imagine' – and seems to have followed him, studying him from a distance: 'It was always amusing to hop from puddle to puddle in the strides of Charlie's hob-nailed boots.' However introductions were eventually broached, Charlie was to encourage and advise Beatrix in the increasingly intricate botanical drawing she was undertaking. As a result, much later in life, she was to engage in serious work dissecting, drawing and classifying fungi, and became an authority. But the discipline was also to prove invaluable in her drawing from nature now.

In the flowering of her talent Beatrix was fortunate, too, in finding in a new governness – Miss Hammond – a woman sensitive to her art. But life back home, in London, was no more social than before – in fact less so once Bertram had been despatched to boarding school. There were long depressing months of loneliness relieved by the drawing – 'I must draw, and when I have a bad time come over me it is a stronger desire than ever' – and by a growing menagerie of imported friends: a pair of mice which she kept hidden in a box, a rabbit who was supposed to live in the garden but spent most of its time on the hearthrug in Beatrix's room, and a hedgehog called Tiggy who was a regular guest at Beatrix's dolls tea parties. They became her constant companions.

Then suddenly, in 1882, when she turned sixteen, the holidays at Dalguise ceased and Beatrix's imaginative life lost its anchor in the real world. The loss so troubled her that when two years later the opportunity arose to re-visit the estate she shied away from it at first, for fear that a changed Dalguise would contradict the precious childhood image in her mind.

Beatrix's pet Benjamin Bunny.

Thursday, May 8th, 1884 – I am afraid there is a chance of going back to Dalguise. I feel an extraordinary dislike to this idea, a childish dislike, but the memory of that home is the only bit of childhood I have left. It was not perfectly happy, childhood's sorrows are sharp while they last, but they are like April showers serving to freshen fields and make the sunshine brighter than before.

We watch the gentle rain on the mown grass in April, and feel a quiet peace and beauty. We feel and hear the roaring storm of November, and find the peace gone, the beauty becomes wild and strange. Then as we struggle on, the thoughts of that peaceful past time of childhood come to us like soft music and a blissful vision through the snow. We do not wish we were back in it, unless we are daily broken-down, for the very good reason that it is impossible for us to do so, but it keeps one up, and there is a vague feeling that one day there will again be rest.

The place is changed now, and many familiar faces are gone, but the greatest change is in myself. I was a child then, I had no idea what the world would be like. I wished to trust myself on the waters and sea . . . Then just as childhood was beginning to shake, we had to go, my first great sorrow. I do not wish to have to repeat it . . . let me keep the past . . .

I could not see it in the same way now, I would rather remember it with the sun sinking, showing, behind the mountains, the purple shadows creeping down the ravines into the valley to meet the white mist rising from the river. Then, an hour or two later, the great harvest-moon rose over the hills, the fairies came out to dance on the smooth turf, the night-jar's eerie cry was heard, the hooting of the owls, the bat flitted round the house, roe-deer's bark sounded from the dark woods, and faint in the distance, then nearer and nearer came the strange wild music of the summer breeze.'

Monday, May 26th: Arrived at Pople's Hotel 5.30. O how homely it seems here, how different to anything I have seen since I left – I went down by the river after tea. The grass is greener, the flowers thicker and finer. It is fancy, but everything seems so much more pleasant here. The sun is warmer and air sharper. Man may spoil a great deal, but he cannot change the everlasting hills, or the mighty river, whose golden waters still flow on at the same measured pace, mysterious, irresistible. There are few more beautiful and wonderful things than a great river. I have seen nothing like it since I left; down to the smell of the pebbles on the shore, it may be drainage, but it brings back pleasant memories.

I remember Home clearer and clearer, I seem to have left it but yesterday. Will it be much changed? How fast the swifts fly here, how clearly the birds sing, how long the twilight lasts!

Tuesday, May 27th: Down over to Dalguise, a forlorn journey, very different to the usual one . . . The place is the same in most ways. It is home. The bridge re-built at Inver, and some new railings on the Duke's land. Some saplings grown, others dead. Here and there a familiar branch fallen, and, on the Dalguise land, things more dilapidated than ever, and some new cows in the fields.

A horrid telegraph wire up to the house through the avenue, a Saw-Mill opposite the house and a pony-van at the back. There are deaths and changes, and the curse of drink is heavy on the land. I see nothing but ruin for the estate. How well I remember it all, yet what has not happened since we left? What may not happen before I see it again if I ever do – I am not in a hurry to do so. It was a most painful time, and I see it most as well with my eyes closed.

As teenager became young woman, Beatrix's ageing parents began increasingly to make demands on her and the desire to escape Bolton Gardens grew stronger daily. By this time, on the pages of her sketchpads, while her animals remained in every structural detail true to nature, anthropomorphism had crept in.

Four-footed creatures walked upright or wore clothes, developed personalities or undertook human tasks. It was a vogue of the time. This was the age of the affably satirical artist Randolph Caldecott; his book, 'The Frog He Would A-wooing Go', had been a big bestseller in 1883. Like Beatrix Potter, Caldecott had honed his art by close copying of nature, by sketching and modelling, and even dissecting birds and animals. And how similar now seem the drawings of Caldecott's frog to Beatrix's later Jeremy Fisher. New influences were bid welcome as Beatrix took a more practical route to escape her parents – financial independence!

By 1891 she was working on drawings to sell – drawings with titles such as 'Rabbits Christmas Party', 'Three Little Mice Sat Down to Spin'. Then, in 1893 while staying at Eastwood, a dower house, near Dunkeld on the River Tay, she decides to share one of her stories with Noel Moore, the son of an erstwhile governess, Annie Moore. It became one of the most famous letters ever written, and it began like this –

> My dear Noel,
>   I don't know what to write to you so I shall tell you a story about four little rabbits whose names were –
>
> > Flopsy,
> > Mopsy,
> > Cotton-tail,
> > and Peter . . .

It was five years before 'The Tale of Peter Rabbit' was published. In 1902 and 1903 followed 'The Tailor of Gloucester' and 'Squirrel Nutkin', two other tales that began in the same way as 'Peter Rabbit'. By then Beatrix had managed to buy Hill Top Farm at Sawrey in the Lake District, the place where she was to resolve her childhood unhappinesses by re-creating and spreading its occasional joys.

One thing that Beatrix had loved about the Scotland of her youth was the realism of life on the farms. She could smell it, see it, feel it in a way that made dull Bolton Gardens seem a clinical sham. Farm people were in touch, and now as a farmer herself (and she became a very successful one at Hill Top), Beatrix had become one of them. Childhood images had at last begun to merge with her own exterior life.

At Hill Top she flourished as at no other time. The next eight years saw her most productive literary period, thirteen books, no fewer than six of them are set in Sawrey village itself. But geographical reference points are poor guidelines to understanding Beatrix Potter's Art. For all her books, wherever they may be

Hill Top Farm at Sawrey in the Lake District, now museumised and made open to the public. Here Beatrix flourished as at no other time.

set, hark back to that childhood vision of the countryside – places and sentiments – made vivid by a little girl's imagination starved of joy. 'I have been laughed at for what I say I can remember; but it is admitted that I can remember quite plainly from one and two years old; not only facts, like learning to walk, but places and sentiments – the way things impressed a very young child.'

These sentiments – her childhood vision – not only permeated each one of her books but lived within her day-to-day, and the local community at Sawrey Village was only too pleased to become a part of her vision too, as this letter to Millie Warne (her publisher) shows:

The 'Ginger and Pickles' book has been causing amusement. It has got a good many views which can be recognised in the village, which is what they like: they are all quite jealous of each other's houses and cats getting into a book. I have been entreated to draw a cat aged twenty 'with no teeth'. The owner seemed to think the 'no teeth' was a curiosity and attraction! I should think the poor old thing must be rather worn out.

A Mr John Taylor was the bedridden owner of the village shop when Beatrix was writing 'Ginger and Pickles'; she dedicated the book –

With very kind regards to old Mr John Taylor, who 'thinks he might pass as a dormouse': (three years in bed and never a grumble!).

In explanation, she wrote this to Louisa Ferguson:

The book was all drawn in the village near my farmhouse, and the village shop is there. Only poor old 'John Dormouse' is dead – just before the book was finished. I was so sorry I could not give him a copy before he died. He was such a funny old man: I thought he might be offended if I made fun of him, so I said I would only draw his shop and not him. And then he said I had drawn his son John [the village carpenter] in another book, with a saw and wagging his tail [John Joiner in 'The Roly-Poly Pudding'], and old John felt jealous of young John. So I said how could I draw him if he would not get up? – and he considered for several days, and then 'sent his respects, and thinks he might pass as a dormouse!' It is considered very like him . . . Also, it is very much like our 'Timothy Baker', but he is not quite so well liked, so everybody is laughing.

At long last, everybody – including Beatrix – was laughing.